SHOULD WE CHANGE
Our
GAME PLAN?

SHOULD WE CHANGE *Our* GAME PLAN?

From Traditional or Contemporary
to Missional and Strategic

George G. Hunter III

Abingdon Press
Nashville

SHOULD WE CHANGE OUR GAME PLAN?
FROM TRADITIONAL OR CONTEMPORARY TO MISSIONAL AND STRATEGIC

Copyright © 2013 by Abingdon Press

This book is printed on acid-free paper.

Library of Congress Cataloging-in-Publication Data has been requested.

ISBN 978-1-4267-6385-4

Scripture quotations are from the Common English Bible. Copyright © 2011 by the Common English Bible. All rights reserved. Used by permission. www.CommonEnglishBible.com.

13 14 15 16 17 18 19 20 21 22—10 9 8 7 6 5 4 3 2 1

MANUFACTURED IN THE UNITED STATES OF AMERICA

To my Ella Fay

I experienced an emotional resurrection when I met her.
We became a team and designed a new game plan,
and life ever since has been more meaningful
and fulfilling than it ever could have been without her.

CONTENTS

Contents

Contents

"SHOULD WE CHANGE OUR GAME PLAN?"

I promise this is not still another book encouraging "traditional" churches to change and become "contemporary." We have enough of those! Nor does this book mainly focus on a church's worship service. We have enough of those books too. Our focus is upon the other 160+ hours of the week, upon who the church is, and who it's people are, and what they do beyond the church's facilities.

So how can you know, without wasting a dozen hours of your life, that this book isn't a bait-and-switch Trojan horse, i.e., a case for "contemporary" by another name? By giving you a peek at one of the book's most important conclusions: many of the most effective churches across the earth do many things that some people view as "contemporary," and they do many things that some people view as "traditional."

But this is where it becomes initially confusing: many of the most effective churches do not merely blend the traditional and contemporary; nor do they do traditional stuff in the same old way; nor do they do contemporary stuff in (what has become) the same

1

fairly old way; and much of what they do is quite beyond the (now) customary thinking in categories like "traditional," "contemporary," and "blended."

Welcome to some different categories. For reasons that this book will unpack, the most viable and contagious churches in the future will be "missional" (or "apostolic") churches, and the most effective among those will be "strategic" local movements. This book is written to urge many church leaders to change from tradition to mission (or from contemporary to missional, or from diversity to missional) and from missional to strategic; and, if I've done my job, to inform a quiet revolution in thousands of churches in the United States and beyond.

Let's imagine a more missional and strategic future through a sports analogy. Years ago, I was leading a seminar in a local church. I had reviewed some of the ways that the church's social context has changed since 1500 and since 1950. Ralph spoke up. He confessed to being an "ESPN addict" and then asked a stimulating question. "Mr. Hunter, I have been reflecting on how the game of basketball has changed since I played in college in the 1950s. You are saying that the 'game' that Christianity plays has changed a lot since the 1950s. So, in our church, should we change our game plan?" Ralph's question has become the title of this book. While I will explain in the next chapter some of the major ways that Christianity's "game" has changed in the last five hundred years, as well as the last fifty or sixty, let's explore Ralph's useful analogy.

* * *

Bob Billingslee Jr. has been the varsity basketball coach for thirty years at old Eastern State University. He succeeded his father, who coached basketball at ESU for thirty-five years. Billingslee Sr. was a traditional, old-school Clair Bee basketball coach; Junior is even more old school. Junior may be the greatest living master of the game as it was played in 1955. He plays two guards, two forwards, and a center; no player is a point guard, shooting guard, small forward, or power forward. You will see his players shooting two-hand from-the-chest set shots, and underhand free throws, and you will not see them dunking the basketball.

Coach Billingslee laments what has "happened to the game" beyond his enclave. The three-point shot, he says, has added "chaos" to the game; the recent custom of intentional fouling in a game's last minutes is "obscene;" the full-court press is "ugly." His team has no weight room, and he does not want one. "Lifting weights makes athletes muscle bound," he declares.

It's not that Billingslee never adjusts to the changing game; he necessarily cooperates with the three-second rule about offensive players occupying "the paint," and, six or eight years ago, he finally let his players step out of the 1950s short shorts and into more contemporary uniforms. Overall, however, he resents what "they" have done to "the gentlemen's game."

For a decade or more, in the extended Billingslee regime, the program was somewhat successful. Eastern's culturally traditional fan base enjoyed "the old game," and the coach actually had a recruiting advantage with players who'd mastered the two-handed set shot and so on. However, both of those populations are vanishing. The team now finishes at the bottom of its conference, and the program is at (or past) a crossroad. But Billingslee and his loyalists are still in denial; "If we just try harder, the winning seasons will return."

Meanwhile, down the street from ESU, you will see the impressive somewhat Gothic edifice of Old East Side Church (where the Billingslee clan has attended for two generations). Old East Side was once the largest church in this college town. The church once reported 2,000 members and, most any Sunday, some 1,200 people attended to hear "great preaching," inspiring choral anthems, and "the best pipe organ in the state." As many people attended the Sunday school, with classes for all ages.

Since that golden era in the 1950s, Old East Side's membership strength has declined, almost every year, relentlessly. While the church still reports seven hundred members, about two hundred people now rattle around in the sanctuary; the Sunday school's attendance has declined even more.

At one level, the reason for the church's decline is absolutely no mystery. Most churches in a given year, Old East Side included, lose 5 to 7 percent of their members per year—as members die or transfer to other churches or become so inactive that their names are removed from the membership roster. Churches grow, generally, as they receive more new people than 5 to 7 percent of their membership total each year. Old East Side, like 80 percent of the nation's churches, is declining because it consistently receives fewer new people than 5 to 7 percent of their membership total, year after year.

There are somewhat deeper reasons why Old East Side is declining. The church once received about seventy new members per year—perhaps thirty by transfer, twenty from the children's confirmation class, and twenty from the community—people professing faith, with no prior church to transfer from.

Several changes disrupted that growth pattern. At some point, the members started having fewer children; a dozen years later, the declining birth rate was reflected in smaller confirmation classes, and the church quietly joined the mainline denominational churches that now retain perhaps half of their children when they became adults.

Meanwhile, the climate for evangelizing pre-Christian people changed and Old East Side did not adapt. Communities became less open to two-by-two visitation evangelism; the Sunday school changed its priority from reaching new people to "nurturing our members;" the Sunday evening service became inwardly focused, ceased reaching new people, and eventually closed shop; the annual revival ran out of steam. In time, the church's leaders and people had lost touch with Christianity's main business. With the changes in the community and the surrounding culture, the opportunities for friendship evangelism and for ministry and conversation with pre-Christian people have significantly increased, but the emerging generation of members was more reluctant than their parent's generation to venture beyond their comfort zone. Meanwhile, many Old East Side members lost confidence in their denomination; they still loved their local church, they saw their friends there, they weren't going anywhere, but they had less incentive to invite nonmembers (potential transfers or potential converts) to become involved.

There are still deeper reasons for Old East Side's stagnation and decline:

1. The church's leaders are aware that their world has changed but, like Coach Billingslee, they do not like the way the game has changed. They believe that the world of their parents and grandparents was a better world than the one they see today, and they prefer the church's language, music, and aesthetics of that period.

2. They choose to perceive the changes in the community around them as a problem rather than an opportunity, as an old community dying rather than a new community being born and yet to be shaped.

3. They choose to perceive the secular world as threatening to the souls of their members, so they have withdrawn much of their presence from the community. They have circled the wagons, and now many of their children are home-schooled or private-schooled, most of their friends are Christians, they confine their shopping to Christian merchants, they exercise at the church rather than the town's health club, they plan to retire in a retirement community that is of, by, and for Christians; they may even fraternize with members of only one political party, and so on.

4. Since the church's leaders have heard, through their grapevine, that the significantly growing churches of the nation

only entertain people, they serve "cheap grace," and they do not develop depth in their people, they only learn from other declining churches and denominations.

5. If Old East Side wants a desirable future, the church is currently on the nonstrategic side of every major issue that this book addresses. This book's purpose is to help such churches find a strategic way forward in their changing secular and increasingly postmodern communities.

* * *

The two case studies, the ESU basketball program and Old East Side Church, are both fictional—although the first is enormously more fictional than the second. As far as I know, no college basketball program is in fact stuck in the two-hand set shot era, and no head coach like Bob Billingslee has secure employment. Consider the main business issue. While more than a few varsity athletic programs may be deficient in the student part of what they want to achieve through their student-athletes, the athlete part is clear. The coach *will* prepare and field a team that is competitive for the game as it is today. The fans, the donors, and the university have ways of insisting!

The profile of Old East Church is much less fictional. Old East Side is a composite of a number of the churches I have studied and observed in half-a-lifetime. In the United States alone, at least two hundred thousand churches roughly fit the Old East Side description. The church is much less clear about their main business than the athletic department down the street.

In some ways, the church's challenge is more difficult than the basketball teams. The church's donors often pay to endow the perpetuation of the church they once experienced faith in, or grew up in, because they love the familiar sounds of Zion, and they doubt that Christianity can be faithfully expressed in other ways. We shall see, however, that Old East Side has an enormously greater opportunity than the ESU basketball team, and it will fulfill that opportunity if, in strategically appropriate ways, it becomes very traditional *and* very current and much more strategic.

The two hypothetical cases of Old East Side Church and the ESU basketball team have at least one thing in common: their respective games have changed. Furthermore, their aesthetic appraisals may be right: their respective games in 1957 may, indeed, have been more honorable and pure. But that is not the time that history has entrusted to these two organizations now.

The test for ESU basketball is competing (like it or not) in an environment of weight-trained athletes executing jump shots, three-point shots, slam dunks, and full-court presses. (Presumably the showboating is still optional!) The test for Old East Side is competing for the hearts and souls of populations with no Christian background or memory, who are not culturally shaped to resonate to the music of Bach or Wesley, with short attention spans, and with hang-ups about organized religion and a dozen other features that confuse Old East Side's leaders.

* * *

Some stagnant and declining churches, however, are *not* especially analogous to the ESU basketball program.

For instance, some churches are analogous to another type of basketball program that one can easily imagine; let's call it Central State University. CSU's coach and his fan base are obsessed with whatever is *new* in college basketball. On defense, he once taught his players to wait at mid-court and then defend man-to-man. Then he decided that a zone defense was the wave of the future. One year, after Arkansas had won two NCAA championships, the coach installed a "forty-minutes-of-hell" full-court press. Later, he coached his players to protect the baseline and force the ball to the corner. Almost every new season has featured a new defensive flavor of the year.

7

On offensive game plans, CSU has covered the full range of basic options—from the set offense, to the motion offense, to a zone offense, to a spread offense. For several years, he wanted his team to run set plays; the next year he called for freelance improvisation on the floor. One year, the coach decided that the Princeton offense was the way to go. Then, when Kentucky won the 2012 NCAA championship, he announced the CSU incarnation of John Calipari's dribble-drive offense.

Unlike Arkansas, Princeton, and Kentucky, however, the CSU coach had not recruited players for the next great scheme, but for the scheme recently abandoned, so players are often expected to perform in systems that they do not fit. For instance, the coach has recently expected his point guards to adopt the hyper-quick, slashing, improvisational style of Rajon Rondo—the problem is that there may be no more Rondos.

Moreover, the CSU coach keeps changing his personal coaching persona. For some years, fans were amused by his emulation of the Bobby Knight in-your-face exchanges with his players; more recently he has become a Roy Williams-suited look-alike. The constant changes have negatively affected CSU's recruiting, performance, and identity. The program lacks continuity and philosophy. And the program never sticks with one approach long enough to become known for it, recruit for it, and become good at it. He has managed to keep his job, however, because the program has cultivated a fan base that likes, cheers for, and now expects novelty.

Alas, the CSU basketball program is analogous to many contemporary churches. Every year, sometimes every season, features new music, new jargon, new celebrative expressions, new trendy topics for the lead pastor's "message". (The word "sermon" is never heard.) And, with increasing frequency, a weekend features a new celebrity speaker, singer, or band. Such churches often succeed in retaining, in some form of church, the generation who prefers to drive something other than their father's Oldsmobile. However, the self-consciously contemporary churches typically have great difficulty helping their attenders graduate from being mere consumers of religious experiences; some trendy churches do not even own the consumerism problem. In any case, the impact of a CSU-type church upon the community's pre-Christian populations is usually negligible.

* * *

Again, many mainline churches are analogous to another possible basketball model. Imagine that the agenda of Western State University's basketball program is now subservient to a wing of the university's faculty, which has engineered a diversity requirement for the recruitment of WSU basketball players. The team must now have at least "one of each." The coach has had no trouble recruiting Blacks and Anglos, but few Hispanics live in the state, and the expectation that he recruit Korean, Caribbean, Inuit, and Native American players for the positions he needs to fill is daunting. The coach has to juggle unusual recruiting challenges; where will he go to find an available, competitive, Pacific Islander point guard?

There are many more such churches than there are basketball teams. A feature of a Christian ethic drives them, a feature that most Christians affirm; most Christians value diversity, and many work and pray for it. When, however, that value trumps all others and inclusiveness is what it is *all* about, typically they neither reach new people nor retain their own young people over time. This dream now drives many denominations; the more this value becomes the ruling priority, the more net decline the denominations experience.

* * *

So underachieving American and European churches are stuck in one of several paradigms that, when elevated to the top priority position, limit their effectiveness in their communities. I have featured three such models that, in shorthand, might be referred to as the Traditionalist, the Contemporary, and the Diversity models.

This book features, for each of these churches and others, some of the known ways forward. Most of the chapters focus on some of the indispensable questions and issues that are the hinges that swing a church in one direction or another. The first chapter, however, summarizes how the game has changed. Every church leader needs to have his or her mind around how our Western mission field has changed and the more specific changes in that mission field to which the church is called to strategically adapt.

HOW THE GAME CHANGED

The introduction featured a basketball analogy to suggest that the game has really changed for American and European churches. Churches once vital and growing did not flex with changing communities, changing populations, and new opportunities, and are now stagnant or declining and facing an undesirable future. Already, many churches that once thrived, like Pan Am or Oldsmobile, are now spent forces; others, like Sears or Kodak, are diminished.

This first chapter provides an overview of *how* the game changed over time. The changes usually came along slowly—for five hundred years. Not much usually happened from one month to the next or from one year to the next; the changes were usually from one decade, or one generation, or one century to the next. The changes were (and are) enormous, but they usually happened slowly enough to explain how, like Rip Van Winkle, most church leaders slept through a revolution.

While I used the game of basketball to suggest that the game has changed, let's turn to the game of football to explain *how* it has changed. Alas, the explanation involves more history than many people are salivating to read. But one cannot really understand where we are today without an overview of how we got here. What follows is more of a briefing than a history, more of a watercolor painting of the main features in bold strokes, rather than the details of an oil painting.

Home Field Advantage . . . for a Thousand Years

For about one thousand years, the Western church was like a football team that played every game at home. Christianity enjoyed a perennial "home-field advantage." Indeed, the church wrote the rules, the church briefed the referees, the crowd was always behind the church. To vary the analogy, the church enjoyed a worldview "monopoly" for many centuries. People viewed reality through a Christianized lens. Christianity was Western society's official and privileged religion. Virtually everyone in Western society was a baptized and catechized Christian.

Historians have named this period "Christendom." It began some time after Constantine adopted Christianity in the Christian movement's fourth century. It essentially lasted, with many shifts, until the events of the fifteenth and sixteenth centuries launched the process of the West's secularization.

The Christendom period was, of course, a mixed achievement. Some populations were never reached. Many populations were under-reached; they had been baptized, and probably "catechized," and were members of a geographic parish. But many became Christians because the local prince or baron did, and he expected his subjects to convert. Many conversions were superficial, and nominal Christianity was often epidemic; many people were never able to follow the Mass in Latin, and they never understood the doctrines. The old folk-religion was driven underground, but it still lived in many people's homes and assumptions. The Christianity of many people was "Christo-pagan;" the old pagan meanings were now attached to the newer Christian words, symbols, and saints.

Many people were only episodically involved in the church's life; in addition to Christmas and Easter, they attended baptisms, weddings, and funerals. (They came to be "hatched, matched, and dispatched!") In time, the parish had thousands of people, or tens of thousands, so the priest's job description was largely confined to the sacraments, leading the mass, and hearing confessions. The faith was domesticated. Søren Kierkegaard was to observe that when everyone is a Christian (in this diluted sense), then probably nobody is the kind of Christian that the early apostles would recognize.

And yet, as the English economic historian R. H. Tawney reminded us, Christendom was a serious attempt to establish a Christian society, in which the will of God might be done on earth "as in Heaven." A serious Christian ethic informed and influenced the society. Vocational guilds were established to ensure that young craftsmen were mentored, and that products and services met standards and were sold at a fair price. In economics, bankers could not charge people excessive interest; usury was a mortal sin. (In Dante's hell, usurers were consigned to one of hell's lowest realms.) Christianity influenced the political realm and achieved a period of relative peace compared to the warfare that followed Christendom's later collapse. The era inspired unspeakably great art, architecture, music, and literature. The era liberated people from much of the evil and magic that had prevailed. The era produced saints.

Locally, in virtually every town and village in Christendom, the parish church served as the center of the people's community. Family members were baptized, married, and buried there. The local parish church likely housed the only books in town and provided some literacy and education. The parish church belonged to people of all classes; alms for the poor were available in hard times. The church was the community's refuge in times of famine or epidemic. The community experienced its social life in the church, from weekly entertainment to holidays and festivals and markets set up in the churchyard.

At every level, from local villages to centers of government, the society at least worked at marching to Christianity's drum; the church influenced every area of life and influenced most of the people of the society. The Christendom experience gave many people a taste of what a good order might be like. But Christendom is now gone with the proverbial wind, and no one has since attempted anything like it on a large scale.

The Game Changers

How did the church lose its home-field advantage in Western society? In general, it happened as secularizing events moved the church from the society's center and toward its margins. Often this move occurred more or less unintentionally, but sometimes intentionally. Consider one example: people, for generations, left land to the church in their wills. In time, the church had acquired extensive land—perhaps as much as a fourth of the land of (what is now) Germany, France, and Britain, with extensive land holdings across much of Western Europe. In one generation or two, regional princes saw the land, organized armies, sacked the monasteries, and seized the land. They said at the time that the land was being "secularized," i.e., removed from the control or influence of the church.

While the secularization of church lands happened consciously and intentionally, the secularization of other areas of Western humanity's life often occurred more or less unconsciously and unintentionally, largely as a result of six sustained events:

I. **The European Renaissance,** led by Erasmus and others, was catalyzed by the rediscovery of ancient Greek philosophy and science. For centuries, Christianity provided the only sophisticated worldview available to the West's peoples; a recovered Greek worldview now introduced pluralism, which became an increasing, more recently a stampeding, feature of Western thought and life. Furthermore, Western humanity's attention substantially shifted from theological and ecclesiastical concerns to humanity's freedom and progress. The line of the Greek sophist Protagoras, "Man is the measure of all things," pointed in a new direction.

II. **The Protestant Reformation** and the **Roman Catholic Counter Reformation**, led by Luther and others, essentially completed the new beginning. People said while they both lived, "Erasmus laid the egg and Luther hatched it." The church was now split. The attention of both churches turned inward—upon renewal and theological clarity, and away from the de facto management of society.

III. The rise of the **Modern Nation-State**, and the **Spirit of Nationalism**, undermined the sense of a common humanity that Christendom had instilled. Europe fragmented big time. *Secular* nations arose that, by design, would no longer act out the script of a church. While Europe had never been innocent of cultural chauvinism and intercultural conflict, the ideology of nationalism magnified this sin by the power of ten. Many peoples now regarded only their own people as fully human and other peoples as something less; this led to unprecedented warfare. Europe and its cultural outposts (like the United States, especially the United States) have never sufficiently recovered.

IV. The significance of the rise of **Secular Cities** cannot be overstated. The very early Christian movement was more contagious in the Roman Empire's cities than in the villages and hinterlands, but in modern times the Christian faith has experienced a more robust challenge in the cities. As many people moved from the countryside to the cities during the Industrial Revolution, they were removed from God's natural revelation. William Blake observed, "Great things are done when men and mountains meet / This is not done by jostling in the street."

V. Most church leaders know at one level that **Empirical Science** has contributed to the West's secularization, but this is such a commonplace insight that church leaders no longer seem to be sensitive to the fact that many of the assumptions of pre-Christian people have been shaped by the influence of science. If empathy is a prerequisite to effective ministry, it might be useful to reintroduce what secularization looks and feels like from referring to just five thinkers:

Galileo, in using his telescope to demonstrate the validity of Copernicus' theory, undermined the traditional view of the cosmos and the earth's place in the cosmos. The sun did not, despite common sense perceptions, revolve around the earth—giving us our days and nights. The earth revolves around the sun, and as the earth rotates on an axis, it gives us our days and nights. And contrary to Western humanity's inherited worldview, neither the earth nor our solar system are even close to being the center of God's universe.

Although Isaac **Newton**, like Galileo, was a devoted Christian, his discovery of the force of gravity undermined the traditional understanding of Providence in the minds of many people. People long believed that the hand of God kept the stars and planets in their orbits, but Newton's *Principia Mathematica* demonstrated that gravity could account for the universe's cohesion.

Charles **Darwin** started out as a Christian (or at least a Deist) and even considered the Anglican priesthood. His discoveries of the principle of natural selection in nature induced doubts, in his own mind, about William Paley's argument for the existence of God from the complexity in creation; for Darwin, natural selection might account for complex life forms. Furthermore, his theory that advanced creatures, including humans, had evolved from more primitive forbears raised questions about people being God's special creatures, created in God's image, just a little lower than the angels. Today, a majority of people in the Western world do not know they are created in God's image, for God's purpose, for lives of worth and dignity, to be stewards of creation, and so on. In the history of Christian evangelism, our predecessors could assume that pre-Christian people already knew that; today, most people do not already assume that they even matter to God.

Karl **Marx** somehow passed off his thought as scientific. His theories changed many people's view of the goal of human history. The goal was no longer the promised kingdom of God—in which people would beat their swords into plowshares, and the will of God would be done on earth as in heaven. The goal of history was now a secular (atheistic) utopia: the "dictatorship of the proletariat" would arise, following the "withering away of the state." Until the crumbling of the U.S.S.R. in 1989, more people probably assumed a Marxist view of history's direction than a Christian view.

Sigmund **Freud** raised questions about religious beliefs and even religious experiences. He was raised a Jew, but became emotionally estranged from the faith of his people. In time, he contended that God is an "illusion"—rooted in the child's need for an omnipotent father, that religion is "wish fulfillment" and an "obsessional neurosis." In his last book, *Moses and Monotheism*, he came to a greater appreciation of the faith of his people, but the overall body of his work contributed to a secular worldview.

VI. The sixth major secularizing event was the European **Enlightenment**, often called "The Age of Reason." The Enlightenment produced the culture of modernity in the Western world and beyond. The Enlightenment was an astonishingly complex ideological and social movement. We cannot do it justice here except to say that the movement propagated eight claims that became widely believed (or assumed), with significant secularizing effects. The Enlightenment generally taught that:

    a. Human beings are *rational.* It is our capacity for rational thinking that separates us from the beasts of the forests, fields, and jungles.

    b. Human beings are intrinsically *good.* The Enlightenment challenged the Christian doctrine of Original Sin. Its thinkers acknowledged that often people do not live and behave like good people, but the cause is the unjust conditions in which people live; establish more just conditions and people will live good lives.

    c. The *Universe* functions with the clockwork precision of a *machine.* For many people, this confidence made God's providential care unnecessary, and made belief in any kind of spiritual realm optional.

    d. Humans can construct *morality on reason* alone; they do not need the church, or God, to tell them what is right and wrong.

e. Humans can construct *societies on reason* alone. Some leaders were even confident that people could build societies that functioned with the clockwork precision of the physical universe.

f. *Science and Education* will liberate the human race from its longstanding problems.

g. Deep down, *all religions are the same* (or are equal). The Enlightenment's philosophy of Natural Religion reached this major conclusion *before* most of the world's religions had been studied!

In addition to those six sustained events, there were other distinct forces dismantling Christendom. (The Industrial Revolution and the rise of universities come to mind.) However, a renewed awareness of the impact of the Renaissance and the Reformation, the influence of Nationalism and Urbanization, and the cognitive shaping of Science and the Enlightenment can help us understand some of the important ways that the game has changed, how the church lost the home-field advantage, and why the world that God entrusts to the Christian movement today is very different from the world in which (say) Anselm, Aquinas, Luther, Wesley, Kierkegaard, Spurgeon, and even C. S. Lewis, Fulton J. Sheen, and Billy Graham once communicated the faith. As Christianity has lost the pervasive influence it once enjoyed, the western world has become increasingly "secular."

The Secular Mission Fields

Secularization has not been a singular monolithic force in Western history; other major events have impacted regional histories, so secularity is not the same everywhere. As secularization engaged a range of cultures, different forms of secularity emerged. Decades ago, Martin Marty profiled three basic forms that Western secularity has taken:[1]

1. Much of Western Europe was experiencing "Utter Secularity." God and the church were attacked for decades by movements seeking to replace Christianity with something else.

2. Great Britain was experiencing "Mere Secularity." God and the Church were ignored as Britain's people became preoccupied with their daily concerns. The Church of England retained a shell of Christendom, but most British people do not think of Christianity as something to which one might be committed.

3. The United States was experiencing "Controlled Secularity." Church attendance remained popular, but many people (and churches) quietly attached American values to Christianity's symbols, and Christianity was made subservient to American culture's agendas.

Professor Marty's typology is still useful after more than forty years, though some things have changed. You can find people who embody any of the three forms anywhere in Western Europe, the United States, or Great Britain—or its cultural outposts like New Zealand, Australia, or Canada. The more aggressive expression of secularity, once more or less quarantined in Western Europe, now has more of a presence in Great Britain and the U.S.A.

Theories of Secularity

Secularization has had its fair share of academic interpreters—historians, sociologists, philosophers, theologians, and the like. Generally, three theories have gained rather wide support.

1. The first theory has largely dominated this chapter so far: as institutional Christianity has lost its once-central role and influence in Western society, Western society has become increasingly secular, and the people have been less influenced by Christianity. Although

some churches are in denial and assume that the game has not changed, this theory is the nearest thing to an informed consensus as you are likely to find for any theory, in any field. As Hendrik Kraemer surveyed Western Europe in the 1950s, he wrote, "The modern world, by its victorious secularism, has domesticated the Church into a 'reservation' for people with religious needs, and the Church has largely accepted this domestication."[2]

2. Alas, some of the early sociologists who reflected on the phenomenon of secularization were ideologues. They forecasted a time when religion would disappear, or nearly so, and people would live in terms of this world alone, with no interest in transcendence. Subsequent Western history did not unfold that way. As the church lost its monopoly, other worldviews moved into the void. Perhaps the earliest seriously secular nation was Germany, but the Germany that the Third Reich hijacked was not a secular rational society in this second sense; occult beliefs and practices had become rampant. More widely, the twentieth century was the most secular century so far (in the sense of the first theory), but communism moved into that void—with the belief that "the dialectical process" was ultimate and cooperating with it was a holy cause. One need look no farther than the line of people outside Lenin's tomb in Red Square to see visual evidence of a de facto religion that once presumed to replace Christianity. Today, across the Western world, something like religious anarchy prevails: popular belief in luck, the dialectic, the "invisible hand," Karma, reincarnation, alien visitations, alien abductions, Big Foot, ghosts, witches, astrology, UFOs, ESP, The Force, the Mayan calendar, crystals, and much more—much of that sometimes inhabiting the same individual!

3. Charles Taylor's recent "greatest book" on secularity develops a third theoretical perspective, which reflects upon a more recent advanced consequence of the secularization process: "The shift to secularity . . . consists, among other things, of a move from a society where belief in God is unchallenged and indeed, unproblematic, to one in which it is understood to be one option among others, and

frequently not the easiest to embrace."[3] Please read that loaded sentence again; that is a game changer!

How Some Churches Responded to the Changed Game

Often, churches have not responded strategically to their new secular setting. One can, after all, sense that the game has really changed and then respond in dysfunctional and counter-productive ways. What follows is a partial litany of bad game plans:

1. Much of the Western church responded to the challenges to the faith with natural theology and Deism. William Paley, for instance, employed the now-famous "watchmaker" analogy; the complex design we can observe in, say, the human hand, implies an Intelligent Designer. Following Darwin, however, many people believed that evolution by natural selection might account for complexity in creation. In time, most of Western culture assumed that one must first become convinced in the existence of a God and then consider whether Christianity's revelation of God might be true. This shift put a greater burden on the back of natural theology than it was originally meant to carry. In Celtic Christianity, for instance, nature was "the second book of God"; faith in Christ frees us to also perceive his signs and footprints in nature—to which pre-regenerate people are often blind. Furthermore, those who did conclude a God from the hints in nature often wound up with Deism—God as an absentee landlord, not the triune God of the Christian revelation.

2. Often the church referred to God in the sense of what Dietrich Bonhoeffer called the "Deus Ex Machina," or the stopgap God. God was assumed to be the cause of events, like lightning, that science could not explain; with Benjamin Franklin's discovery of lightning's cause, God was edged out of the lightning business. Or God was the one people turned to for help when they could not

help themselves; then as people could help themselves more and more through medical advances and in other ways, they called on God for help less and less. Of course, "the God of the Gaps" was never the Biblical God, who will be known as Lord, or perhaps not known at all.

3. Sometimes, to fend off secularization, the churches reduced Christianity's scope. The focus was upon people's souls and family life and much less upon concerns like justice or peace. Several traditions executed this strategy rather effectively, but at the cost of ignoring much of the Bible, and no longer demonstrating Christianity's redemptive relevance to all of life.

4. The churches, in many places, came to resemble football or basketball teams that play "not to lose." They circled the wagons, private-schooled or homeschooled their kids, went to Christian colleges for Christians only, shopped with Christian merchants, socialized only with other Christians, and planned to retire in a community with other Christians only. The purpose was no longer to reach lost people but to protect the church's people from the city's sins, from dangerous ideas and from the secular people who aren't like good church people. Such a strategy looks good, in part because the church playing not to lose can easily identify specific things to do (or not do). However, in the long run, the churches often lose more of their members and their children than if they were giving their kids and members the experience of a church that plays to win. When their children become adults, less than half will still be in a church, at least of that tradition; some play-not-to-lose church traditions lose 70 percent of their kids.

5. In time, many churches have withdrawn their presence from the community; they are neither of the world nor in the world. Since churches lose 5 to 7 percent of their people per year, and since their presence with pre-Christian people is a prerequisite to reaching them, the church's membership strength is declining. It may attempt some impersonal approaches to evangelism for a while, like tracts,

mailings, or advertising; then, when the community's people fail to become Christians, it is somehow their fault.

6. Eventually, the church that no longer knows many lost people now no longer understands them. I have been in many churches where the leaders have no idea what lost secular people are like; they have heard rumors, and they have some (negative) impressions, but they have no "intelligence" that could inform a strategy of ministry and outreach. Like in any sport, you need to scout the other team; but unlike any sport, if we win then they win too.

Secularization Has Produced "Secular People"

The major outcome of secularization, of course, is "secular people." I have always known something about this, firsthand. I was raised in a fairly secular home in Miami, Florida. I experienced faith my senior year in high school; my mom and dad became Christians after I did. Somehow, as a child, I learned the Ten Commandments and the Lord's Prayer, and we could have told a pollster the name of the church we stayed away from! But I was clueless; I knew virtually nothing. At high school baseball practice one day, I asked the coach a question. To him, the answer was an obvious yes; he responded with a rhetorical question: "Is the pope Catholic?" I thought so, but I was not sure!

I experienced second birth and the beginning of a new life the summer between my junior and senior years. The experience clarified my identity and made me more intellectual and more compassionate. Within months I believed that I was called into ministry—with some role in evangelism and mission. After four years at a Methodist college in Florida and two years in divinity school, I spent the summer of 1962 in ministry to people of Muscle Beach, in Southern California. Most of the beach's populations, the muscle crowd, the surfers, the beatniks, the gay community, and others were even more secular than I had been. Most of them could kind of recall a couple of the commandments, but often they did not even recognize the Lord's Prayer, and often they could not tell me the name of the church their parents or grandparents stayed away from.

Although I had been fairly secular myself, the reading I had done about secularization was historical and theoretical. My new friends provided names and faces and specific life experiences for understanding three generalizations about secular people:

☐ As the church lost the privilege of automatic influence with most of the people in the Western world, we experienced the rise of more and more people who had never been substantially influenced by the Christian faith in any viable form.

☐ In time, we experienced the rise and multiplication of people with no Christian background, no Christian memory, and no church to "return" to.

☐ All of our communities now are inhabited by more and more people who have no idea what we Christians are talking about.

The experience at Muscle Beach rubbed my face in questions and issues I have been dealing with ever since. After two degrees in theology, I did a PhD in Communication Studies at Northwestern University to understand from as many perspectives as possible the communication of the meaning of Christianity's message to secular populations. I continued interviewing secular people and converts out of secularity, and I began finding and studying churches that reach secular people. Somewhere along the way, I discovered Donald Soper's *The Advocacy of the Gospel*,[4] in which he reflected upon his long experience in speaking to secular audiences in London's famous open-air forums. In time, he befriended me and became my first mentor in these matters.

Gradually, I developed a ten-point profile of how, generally, majority populations changed from the experience of secularity. While secular pre-Christian people are all individuals, and no two are exactly alike, and some features of the profile will be more prominent, for example, in Western Europe than in the British Isles or North America, the following points will help us understand most secular people. (The first four points are rooted in Soper's pioneering reflection.) After each point, I will suggest at least one strategic implication.

A Profile of Secular People

1. Lord Soper observed a change **from knowledge to ignorance** of basic Christianity in his open-air crowds. Until fairly recent times, even the nonliterate people of a European village were immersed in the catechism, and with the frescos or stained-glass windows as visual aids, they told their children the story of God's saving involvement with the human race. They knew many of the teachings of Jesus and some of the faith's doctrines. By comparison, many educated people today are "ignostics." They are not usually agnostics, or atheists (they are usually Deists or Pantheists), but we cannot presuppose that they know much about the faith that we can build on.

I have observed some variations of the "ignosticism" problem. Some people are misinformed about basic Christianity; they may have much to unlearn. Sometimes people have mistaken a form of folk-religion (like Irish religious folklore or American civil religion) for Christianity. Sometimes people already believe in, and practice, a domesticated form of the Christian faith; Christians are now defined as nice people who attend church, live a clean life, and have a daily devotion. Sometimes people assume that *whatever* they believe must be Christianity. (See the "Baby Jesus prayer" in the movie *Talladega Nights* for an amusing example: Ricky Bobby prefers the Baby Jesus to any adult version, another family member thinks of Jesus as a Ninja warrior, another sees Jesus as the lead singer in a rock band, and so on.)

One strategic response to ignostics is the ministry of instruction; catechesis has become indispensable once again. One cannot reasonably invite people to accept the gospel and begin living by its ethic before they know what it is. Soper used to say that an advocate to secular people would spend his or her whole life explaining basic Christianity—what it claims, stands for, and offers, rather than what they take it to be. Willow Creek's early leaders discovered they had to teach Christianity 101.

2. Western pre-Christian populations have shifted, mainly in the last century or two, **from a death orientation to a life orientation.** For at least sixteen centuries, the Christian movement served populations that were hounded by famines, plagues, epidemics, wars, high infant mortality, and short life expectancy. Medical science had not yet advanced, so every sickness was a crisis. Mortuary science had not yet surfaced, so the deceased remained in the home until the funeral; people often lived "cheek by jowl" with death, and everyone knew the stench of death. Bertrand Russell famously observed that until recent times, most serious thinking was about death. Most people, understandably, feared death and craved life after death. The faith based on the resurrection of Jesus was obviously relevant. For many people, going to heaven appeared to be their sole motive for accepting Christianity.

To a significant degree, much of that has changed. Immunization has tamed most epidemics, modern medicine now cures or controls most sicknesses, getting sick is usually more of an inconvenience than a crisis. Mortuary science now masks some of the reality of death; someone remarked at a recent visitation, "I have never seen him look better!" Life insurance professionals tell us that many people live in denial that they will die.

Consequently, people today are much less likely than their forbears to be thinking about death and asking about life after death, most of the time. They are more likely to be asking questions about the meaning of life, discovering a worthy purpose for their life, living a significant life, and about real life this side of death. Since the gospel is even more about such issues than about death and heaven, churches can learn to engage the changed harvest with new relevance and power.

3. One very major change in Western populations has been a **shift from guilt to doubt** as the most common and obvious feature that a Christian advocate would meet in pre-Christian people. For most of Christianity's history in the West, people were acutely aware that they had not always obeyed God's Law, and they sought forgiveness. Christian theology is clear that people are sinners, and in a diluted form, many people feel guilty; but in the age of pop psychology, those guilt feelings are redefined as the problem.

Soper observed that *doubt* is now the most common and obvious feature we meet in pre-Christian people. We can, from what we discussed above, partly understand why. Ever since the Renaissance introduced pluralism, people have known there are alternative explanations of reality. And from the percolation of ideas from Galileo, Newton, Darwin, Marx, Freud, and others, many people have more questions and doubts than they know what to do with. Sometimes their doubts are involuntary; they don't want them, but they've got them anyway.

The most indispensable strategic response to people's doubts is the ministry of conversation. There is probably no shortcut, with many people, to a period of honest dialogue, involving multiple conversations, in response to their questions and doubts. Sometimes we help them clarify their doubts and name them; often, like the demons in the New Testament, to name them helps to cast them out or reduce their power. Since Christianity is a redemptive approach to the whole of life, we can draw from its wisdom in response to most any question. (If a question stumps us, we admit it, and then we care enough to do our homework for the next conversation.) If a person has many doubts, the task can seem formidable. Fortunately, most people do not need all of their doubts resolved, just enough of them to discover that the Christian possibility for life is supported by some good reasons. Typically, when several doubts are resolved, most of the others seem to melt or lose their power.

4. Another major shift is **from a conscious need for what Christianity offers to curiosity about Christians** and Christianity and (increasingly) other religions, philosophies, and worldviews. One reason why people see less need for Christianity is because the Christianity they may have been exposed to does not meaningfully address some of humanity's major struggles—such as sexuality or war or injustice.

But Lord Soper discovered the pretty good news is that pluralism produces curiosity, and more recently people are curious about the *credibility* of Christians and the church. My own interview research has discovered that this curiosity can focus in one (or more) of three ways: Some people wonder whether we really believe what we say we believe; some people wonder whether we live by what we believe; some people wonder whether what we live by makes much difference. One strategic response is to bring people into fellowship and conversation with some of our most credible Christians and with new converts whom they knew "BC." Another is to involve them in the life of worship that is culturally indigenous to them and with outreach ministries to populations they may already have a heart for.

5. Robert Schuller was the outreach pioneer who helped the church discover that a great many secular people have **issues around self-esteem**. The specific issue is usually low self-esteem, but it can be grandiose self-esteem or volatile self-esteem. Many people have no conscious reason to believe in themselves; they cannot affirm the person who looks back from the mirror when they comb their hair.

Our strategic responses involve sharing the meaning of three of our most profound doctrines: (a) Our dignity is rooted in God's creation of us, in God's image. (b) Our lives are justified by God's grace, not by any merit within us—except that Jesus considered us worth dying for. (c) We begin to discover our identity and purpose as we become followers of Jesus Christ, living by his will and no longer our own.

6. Many secular **people experience their life as out of control.** When the lives of the West's people were embedded in the life of clans and local communities, the society was more of a "we" culture than a "me" culture; the norms and expectations for people's lives were clear, and to some degree, the people of the family, clan, and village monitored and supported the lives of each other. With urbanization and secularization came freedom; people now made many choices that were informed by no experience-based wisdom, and perhaps no one now monitored their lives; indeed societies now seemed indifferent to how one lived. Some people have flourished in such freedom; many other people have languished or self-destructed with such freedom. Some of their choices, once made, take over; the people are deceived, hooked by, and become pathologically dependent upon mysterious powers that are bigger than they are. Many people, for instance, are now addicted to alcohol or to other drugs or to gambling; every community has more people whose lives are out of control around addiction than ever before. Other people's lives are out of control around a range of obsessions and compulsions.

Part of the church's strategic response is providing ministries for out-of-control people. Another is prophetic advocacy in opposition to the cartels and other evil systems that profit through the exploitation of people's weaknesses. Ultimately, however, we invite people to accept and follow Jesus as Lord within his alternative community; they discover, "The one who is in you is greater than the one who is in the world."

7. Many secular **people experience the world as more out of control** than premodern people did. Peoples in medieval times experienced problems, of course, and some of these problems—like some contagious diseases, have been largely eradicated. Natural disasters threatened people then, as today. But in secularization, when the church lost the influence it once exercised in society, nation-

states and (more recently) multinational corporations became laws unto themselves. Western society entered an era of unprecedented warfare. Nazis, then communists, then Islamists launched projects for global domination. The threat of nuclear, chemical, and biological warfare upped the ante. More recently still, the big banks and the Great Recession have caused widespread anxiety, loss, and uncertainty. This is being written two days after a young gunman shot dozens of people in a movie theater in Aurora, Colorado; this has reminded people once again that hand-held "weapons of mass destruction" are out of control. We could go on. In many ways, secular people experience history as an endless series of large-scale shocks, surprises, and threats; as one fellow commented, "It's like nobody is in charge!"

In some ways, the possibility of the church's strategic response is less than in Christendom. The church is now fairly marginalized and fairly ignored in secular human affairs. (In the medium-sized city where I live, Lexington, Kentucky, the pastor of our church was elected a United Methodist bishop; the event warranted a single-column report on page five of the local newspaper.) The church's people, however, have a somewhat greater opportunity to participate in the age of networks and coalitions and cooperate with movements that share some of our goals (if not our theology). And, populations that no longer remember where history is supposed to be moving have the inalienable right to know about the Christian hope of a promised kingdom of God, in which the will of God will be done on earth.

8. With the breakdown of village life and group identity and the rise of individualism, a pathology has spread that no one predicted. Vast numbers of **people are self-preoccupied, self-absorbed, and narcissistic.** The American Psychiatric Association has considered the removal of "narcissism" from its *Diagnostic and Statistical Manual of Mental Disorders*, its book on personality disorders—not because it is not a disorder, but because it is now so widespread. We also often observe collective narcissism— as when a team or a nation assumes,

"We are the greatest." One widespread outcome of unprecedented narcissism is an unprecedented sense of entitlement; professors, for instance, are repeatedly astonished at the research papers whose writers expect an A.

Informed Christianity is entrusted with perspectives on narcissism that all people need. The problem is rooted in Original Sin, i.e., the deep tendency within fallen human beings to take the place of God—assuming that the world revolves around "me" and "us." Martin Luther rhetorically defined Original Sin as "the heart all curled up inside itself." Christianity's doctrine of Atonement, especially the "subjective" theory propounded by medieval theologian Abelard, is Christianity's good news for narcissism: The Love that dies for us on a cross is the only power in the universe greater than our self-love; that Love can reach deeply within us and pull us out of ourselves and reconcile us to God, others, and nature and restore our true selves. Christianity is also entrusted with the antidote to entitlement; Paul and Augustine especially taught us that life is by grace, and that everything we have is "received."

9. Most secular **people are culturally estranged from the church.** They experience the style, language, architecture, aesthetics, and music of traditional churches as expressing a museum-like quality, like their grandfather's Oldsmobile times ten. (Yesterday, my wife and I visited an exhibit of classic cars. We admired a 1930 Packard Deluxe Eight Roadster, and a '57 Chevrolet Bel-Air, and more. One fellow represented the several people I briefly visited with: he admired the cars and said he attends Keeneland's classic car show every summer, but he'd rather drive his 2011 Buick.) The more contemporary churches do connect with secular people somewhat better, and they may present a more celebrative, even entertaining, experience. But a thoughtful unchurched visitor may experience such a church as stuck in the 1970s or inordinately centered on the pastor's charisma or more superficial than a classic liturgy—the most recent Christmas praise chorus may not compare all that favorably to Handel's *Messiah*.

The Christian movement has more experience addressing this kind of challenge than any other. In every mission field, including the secular West today, the contagious Christianity that spreads and produces its fair share of apostles, prophets, saints, and martyrs is indigenous to the culture—translating the faith into the style, language, and aesthetics of the target population.

10. While most secular people have never been substantially influenced by the Christian faith, they have had some **superficial exposure** to Christianity—usually to a diluted form, often from TV, against which they are now immunized. They have a shared perception (often from rumor rather than firsthand) of Christianity as boring, irrelevant, and untrue (or no more true than any other religion or philosophy).

A church's ongoing strategic challenge is to find ways to make their expression of the faith interesting and relevant, to make its truth claims clear, and to let people in on how we see life and the world different through the lenses those truths provide.

The Game Is Changing . . . Again

The Enlightenment swaggered into Western history with enormous confidence in human reason and the brave new world that reason would create. The Enlightenment produced the cultural ethos of "modernity," or the "modern world."

More recently, however, another current has surged in Western life. A growing number of people have experienced the Enlightenment as a failed project; they perceive most of its teachings as untrue, most of its promises as unfulfilled, never to be fulfilled. People who have given up on the Enlightenment and the most recent generation or two who never drank its heady wine at all are called "postmodern."

In recent history many people have simply experienced the Enlightenment as the ideological equivalent of the Wizard of Oz. How that happened involves a very complex story, with many subplots. But some of what postmodernity means can be profiled by returning to the eight teachings of the Enlightenment that were featured above:

☐ From the experiences of the twentieth century, including two world wars, the Holocaust, and the rise and fall of Soviet communism, many people take a more nuanced approach to understanding human nature. The Enlightenment's view of humans as fundamentally rational and good has been exposed as a discredited, naïve, Pollyanna doctrine.

☐ The scientific discoveries of unpredictability and mystery at the microscopic level have led to a less mechanistic understanding of the universe at every level.

☐ Postmodern people are less confident that rational leaders can construct sufficient moralities or societies by reason alone, for no more profound reason than that in more than two centuries no one has achieved it yet.

☐ With a postmodern mood, there is much less confidence in the utopian promises around what science and education would deliver.

☐ Virtually no one now believes that progress is inevitable; it may be possible, but is not assured.

Alas, the Enlightenment teaching that all religions are fundamentally the same is still widely believed, or assumed. The natural religion philosophers had conjectured that while the world's religions look very different at the surface, the deeper down you go in each, the more similar they become; so all religions, presumably, are rooted in the same human religious consciousness. The doctrine was especially advocated during the warfare in Europe, wars ostensibly over religion, that followed Christendom's demise. They seem to have believed that if they could convince Europe's nationalistic leaders that their peoples' religious differences were cosmetic, peace would return. But, as Peter Berger wrote in a 2012 blog, "History is not an ongoing academic seminar."[5] The kings ignored the philosophers, as usual.

While the philosophers were mainly concerned about Protestants of several stripes fighting (or persecuting) Catholics and each other, an important seed had been planted and was now germinating. In time, they taught that presumably all religions, not merely traditions with Christianity, are essentially the same—a conclusion reached without much actual study of Hinduism, Buddhism, Islam, and others.

Here, the Enlightenment was wrong by about 180 degrees. The more recent, and more substantial, study of religions now demonstrates that the major religions are *most alike at the surface;* they tend to have priests, sacred writings and buildings, rites of passage, and so on. The deeper we go in the study of the great religious traditions, the more *different* they are; they represent mutually incompatible core worldviews. One reason to say that Christianity is unique is that every major religious tradition is unique!

Insights about Postmodern Secular People

In any case, except for the Enlightenment's theory about religions, more and more people have abandoned the Enlightenment and are, therefore, postmodern. Generally speaking, we are not yet as clear about what postmodernity is as we are clear about what is it is not: it is not modernity. There are some things that we can already generalize about many, if not most, postmodern people. (Understand, this is only one category—like birth order theory or

Myers-Briggs personality type theory—that helps us understand people. Such a theory may account for 15 percent of who someone is; people are unique individuals. The knowledge of several theories, however, can help us discover how someone is different from their peers.)

For one thing, postmodern people seem to root or base their conscious identity in ways different from their forbears. Premodern people, from clan, tribal, and village cultures said, "I belong, therefore I am." With the Enlightenment and Descartes, modern people said, "I think, therefore I am." Many postmodern people seem to root their identity in one or more of the following ways:

"I feel, therefore I am."

"I disobey, therefore I am."

"I doubt, therefore I am."

"I disagree, therefore I am."

"I choose, therefore I am."

"I am connected, therefore I am."

"I shop, therefore I am."

"I look good, therefore I am."

"I belong, therefore I am." (Welcome to the new peer-based tribalism.)

Author and theologian Leonard Sweet has characterized post-modern people as:[6]

Experiential

Participatory

Image Rich

Connective

I have learned, in interviews with postmodern people that if they come to church, they are more interested in experiencing God than just learning about God. Again, they do not come to church and just sit and listen because they do not (by choice) go anywhere and just sit and listen; if they do not get involved, they won't be back. And one cannot help but observe their hyper-connectivity—calling, e-mailing, texting, and tweeting the people in their network very regularly!

I think I have perceived other features that characterize many postmodern people, if not a majority, compared to people stuck in modernity:

They may be closer to nature and nature's creatures.

They may be more open to mystery and spirituality.

They may be more multisensory—taking in data through all the senses.

They may assume that truth is relative.

They may have shorter attention spans and expect more frequent stimulation.

They may be much more right brained than modernist rationalists.

They may need, and hunger for, community.

As the first generation widely aware of the limitations of words, they may rely on their favored music as the preferred language that speaks to their hearts.

Perhaps the most exasperating feature of many postmodern people is their subjectivity; their postmodern "software" has scripted them to redefine almost everything, including Christianity, to suit themselves. Since at least some people have disengaged from the Enlightenment for a century or more, this has been going on for a long time. Several very public examples should make this clear.

The first amendment to the U.S. Constitution, which provides, "Congress shall make no law respecting an establishment of religion," originally meant that the new nation would not have a national or "established" church—like most of the European countries; a hundred coalitions and pressure groups have added meanings to the amendment to suit themselves. The second amendment, which grants "the right to bear arms," originally referred to the constitutional rights of the states to have their own militias; that original meaning is now usually ignored by most of the people who have added everything that they want the second amendment to mean. Again, the sustained campaign to recognize same-sex marriage is rooted in the postmodern assumed freedom to make marriage (and everything else) mean whatever we want it to mean.

Space does not permit an expose of the many "sects" who have attached their own preferred meanings to Christian terms, symbols, and texts. Christianity has faced this problem ever since the early second century of the Christian movement. The gnostics adopted Christianity's language and claimed to represent a new and improved version of Christianity. But Irenaeus exposed their game. He demonstrated that they attached different meanings to Christianity's words, and he contended that the meanings matter much more than the words. In short, if their meanings are different, it is a different religion or philosophy, despite their adoption of Christian clothing.

Alas, the churches are not immune from this semantic affliction. To cite a public example, in the campaign for the 2012 Republican presidential nomination, Rep. Michelle Bachman was asked if she affirmed the biblical teaching that wives should submit to their husbands. She replied that, yes, in her family "submission means respect," and she professed great respect for her husband. Many church people at least sometimes indulge in the luxury of Christianity meaning whatever they want it to mean! I hope I never have to endure another Bible study where the first question (often the only question) is, "What does this verse mean to you?"

That is not an irrelevant question, because every Christian needs to internalize the meaning of the faith and express some of that meaning in their own words, but the question should come last, or at least *after* learning what the text or truth claim meant originally. In the ministry of witness with pre-Christian people, it is especially our challenge to teach what the faith means, rather than whatever some folks take it to mean.

So, welcome to the new Western mission field. The game has changed and the playing field has changed. Meanwhile, the leaders of Old East Side Church have ignored the changes in the game and the playing field. Indeed, they have even forgotten that the game is supposed to be played on the field. That is, they have forgotten that the true church is a mission whose primary calling is to join the Holy Spirit in finding, loving, serving, and reaching lost people who need to be found; if this does not at least begin on the target population's turf, it isn't likely to happen at all. The church's people seem to assume that the game is mainly about being on the squad and wearing the uniform and learning the playbook and attending the weekly team meetings to listen to the coach teach and to be inspired by the cheerleaders, without getting around to actually playing the game.

The next chapter moves every player from the bench to the playing field.

Chapter Two

THE ONCE AND FUTURE CHRISTIAN LAY MOVEMENT

One day in early May of 2012, I was driving out of northwest Florida into southern Alabama. I was still experiencing the enthusiasm from the recent NCAA basketball tournament that our team in Lexington, Kentucky, had won. I stopped at the Alabama welcome station. The charming woman at the facility asked me, "Now, who are you, and where are you from?" I replied, "I am George, from Kentucky, home of this year's national championship basketball team." Then I asked, "Who are you, and where are you from?" I will never forget her reply: "I am Martha, from Alabama, home of the national champion football team—this year, last year, and the year before!"

In medieval terms, I was "hoisted on my own petard!" An hour later, approaching Montgomery, I was still amused from the experience. I got in touch once again with what the cultural anthropologists tell us: in our post-industrial and cosmopolitan age, we are not as far from tribalism as we think we are.

Many of our churches, especially, function in a kind of tribal culture—specifically a dysfunctional tribal culture, of one kind or another, that is unwittingly driving the gradual decline and fall of the tribe.

So, can the leaders of Old East Side Church (and the other types) get their act together? While the church's name is fiction—it represents the nonfiction reality that at least eight out of ten traditional churches in North America are declining in membership strength year after year. At one level, the reasons for Old East Side's decline are simple. The church loses from 5 to 7 percent of its members per year. Each year, some members die, some transfer their membership to another church, and some just drop out and their names are removed from the roster. (Typically, the names removed from the roll this year actually departed several years ago.)

Since Old East Side is receiving fewer new people each year than it is losing to death, transfer, and reversion, the church is experiencing net membership decline. And they are not so much losing more people than they used to (although aging congregations lose more people to death each year); mainly they now receive fewer new people, year by year, than it takes to replace the 5 to 7 percent that they lose. If Old East Side's leaders are not in denial about their church's decline, they typically regard their decline as a profound mystery; but at the level of Math 101, the cause is pretty simple.

Remarkably, Old East Side is declining while the surrounding community is a biblical harvest. With the secularization of the Western world in the last several centuries, and the church's loss of the religious "monopoly" it once enjoyed, many other religions, philosophies, and ideologies have occupied what was once Christianity's turf. The United States has become the most multi-religious industrial nation on earth; religious anarchy has quietly invaded our communities; the church is in an apostolic time once again!

Meanwhile, many of Old East Side's neighbors are looking for life but in all the wrong places. Often serially, they turn to astrology or spiritualism or luck or the dialectic of Marxism or the invisible hand of capitalism or Hinduism's karma or New Age or drugs or something else that claims ultimacy— to root their identities, to justify their lives, to make sense of their life and the world, to connect to transcendence. Amidst this biblical harvest, Christianity offers what the world needs and is searching for, but Old East Side isn't offering it. Old East Side's "don't ask, don't tell" approach to evangelism fails to engage very many of the city's people who are active seekers, much less the indifferent people and the skeptical people.

"The King and His Court"

At deeper levels, there are two less visible causes that virtually ensure that Old East Side Church will receive fewer people than it loses, which makes the church's future problematic. The first of these deeper causes, the focus of this chapter, is the "clergy-laity heresy." Most Christians have heard about it before, but it is no mere theological abstraction; it is an entrenched pathology in over 90 percent of our churches. To experience what it is like, with some objectivity, let me indulge in an analogy from the sport I loved most in my playing days—men's fast-pitch softball.

One summer evening in Miami, Florida, in the late 1950s, I watched a performance of "The King and His Court." They were a four-man softball team (pitcher, catcher, shortstop, and first baseman) that began on a dare in Walla Walla, Washington, in 1946. With great local fanfare, they beat the best local nine-man team 7-0. Their pitcher, Eddie Feigner, pitched a perfect game and struck out nineteen batters; one opposing batter grounded to shortstop, another to the first baseman. The team's reputation kind of went viral long before there was an Internet. They began traveling the nation, and the world, playing local all-star teams.

Feigner became an entertainer-legend. People came to see him strike their guys out—pitching up to 104 mph (from forty-six feet!), with surprise pitches from behind his back, between his legs, kneeling, blindfolded, and from second base—each pitch preceded by one or more of Feigner's "1001 Motions." In 1967, when Feigner was forty-two, the team played a charity softball game against major league baseball players. Feigner struck out Willie Mays, Willie McCovey, Brooks Robinson, Roberto Clemente, Maury Wills, and Harmon Killebrew. In a row.

The King and His Court, wearing their red, white, and blue uniforms, toured for years. Their website reports that they played before more than twenty million fans, in over 4,400 cities, in over 100 countries. Feigner recorded over 9,700 wins, struck out over 141,000 batters, and threw 930 no-hitters. In time, other four-man teams tried to imitate their success. But, like there has been only one Harlem Globetrotters, so there was only one King and His Court. It was a memorable experience to see four men doing the job of nine (actually one main performer and three fairly anonymous assistants).[1]

The King and His Court made it look so easy, it seemed like any strong pitcher, with any three quick, good-hitting, good-fielding buddies, could duplicate their achievement, but no one else pulled it off, ever. I think I understand two reasons why. First, there was only one Eddie Feigner. Second, it is not reasonable to expect, except for entertainment and with a very cooperative umpire,[2] one guy with three assistants to compete in a game designed for nine-player teams. (Furthermore, it would make even less sense to recruit a softball squad of twenty, to then play only four players, while the other sixteen attended team meetings, practiced daily, but only cheered from the bench during games. Long term, you couldn't even keep much of a team with that game plan.)

At this point, the analogy between sport and church gets thin, because every team in every sport has fewer players than most churches. Many churches are analogous to a fantasy sports team of one hundred players, or one thousand players, or more, suited up for a mission that was originally designed for *no one* to be sitting on the sideline. One towering reason for Old East Side's decline is because for years the "players," say 98 percent, have been only attending team meetings and supporting the pastor and his court, without ever getting into the game. Fortunately, some biblical and historical perspective can liberate us from the paradigm we are so used to, to see the church's new and awesome opportunity in clearer perspective.

Early Christianity Was a <u>Lay</u> Movement

Let's depart from the softball analogy and state it bluntly. No one in the very early Christian movement was a "priest" in the sense that Israel had priests. Furthermore, no one in the period recorded in the New Testament was "ordained" in the sense that any Christian tradition now means. All disciples were called to be "the salt of the earth" and the "light of the world." The whole church was "a royal priesthood;" the risen Christ was the one "High Priest." The new people of God engaged in ministries in and beyond their house churches, based on the spiritual gifts that the Holy Spirit entrusted to each follower of Christ; both men and women were deployed in ministry. As a lay movement, Christianity exploded across the Judean hills and, in time, won a majority of the people of the Roman Empire's cities by persuasion alone.

For at least a century, the movement was lay driven with no clergy. The movement slowly started ordaining some of its leaders in response to challenges they faced from other "teams" on the playing field. The mystery religions had priests, so the church's game plan changed and churches began ordaining priests. Gnosticism challenged Christianity, adopted Christianity's language, and presented itself as a new and improved version of Christianity, so the church began ordaining bishops to ensure the integrity of "the faith once delivered to the saints."

With some people now in priestly and episcopal roles, the church did, indeed, compete more effectively in the ancient world's religious marketplace. The priests seem to have functioned like playing-coaches for their team. The movement continued expanding through a lay apostolate, with some regional variations, for another century. Only gradually did the local priest come to resemble Eddie Feigner. Eventually, however, the churches came to assume that most of the ministry that matters was assigned to the religious professionals; the laity were spectators and beneficiaries of the grace that was mediated through the priests.

Hierarchical Christianity and Lay Religious Orders

Eventually, through the cumulative effect of a hundred little changes, Christianity came to be mostly about the priesthood. Ignatius wrote, "The church consists of the bishop and his clergy." When the bishops met in council, they became the channel of the Holy Spirit. In time, a hierarchy emerged—priests, bishops, archbishop, cardinals, and the pope. Even though the second-century church had remembered the original apostles by their first name only, title inflation moved in. Some leaders with titles, such as bishops Augustine and Patrick, Anselm the Archbishop of Canterbury, and Pope Gregory the Great were absolute giants, and all Christians today are their debtors. Occasional greatness aside, however, hierarchical institutional Christianity became introverted and self-aggrandizing, and sometimes corrupt and worldly.

The good news is that some laity perceived the pathology and believed that laypeople could reform the church. Lay movements like the Cathars, the Waldensians, the Lollards, and the Franciscans returned to the Scriptures, recovered simpler and more devoted Christian lives, and served and preached to people in the communities beyond the churches. In time, more and more lay religious orders emerged to sidestep institutional Christianity's introversion and take the faith to the people.

I once had a brief memorable experience with one of these many orders. One summer day, I was driving on a two-lane state road through a hot, arid, destitute section of the Southwest. I saw occasional shacks and barefoot children. For at least thirty miles, I noticed no churches along that road. Then, to the right, I saw eight or ten nuns visiting with children. Two nuns and a dozen children were playing a game. Then I read the sign across their simple one-story facility: Missionary Sisters of the Precious Blood.

I turned in their driveway and visited with several nuns. I learned that their order began in 1885 in South Africa, when an abbot was inspired to deploy devoted Christian women to bring Christ to tribal Africans. I learned that their order spread to sixteen countries on four continents. They began their work in the United States in the 1930s. One nun shared their motto, "No talent too humble or none too hidden for the glory of God." This convent was, indeed, the only Christian presence within fifty miles or more. They told me that they minister to children and their families, to addicts, and to developmentally challenged adults. In the United States, their order serves a number of First Nation peoples. Many of the order's nuns are trained as nurses, social workers, or teachers. They have built many small hospitals in remote underserved areas.

The Missionary Sisters of the Precious Blood have a lot of company within the Roman Catholic Church. One website reports that that there are 1,262 religious orders fully recognized by the Vatican. There may be twice that number of orders that are not yet fully recognized; I am told that no one knows exactly how many. A joke suggests that this is the first of five things that even God may not know: "God does not know how many Roman Catholic mission orders there are. God does not know who is running the Southern Baptist Convention. God does not know what the Methodists are doing, what the Presbyterians are thinking, or what the Pentecostals are saying!"

Most of the orders are lay orders; about half are women's orders. Some are cloistered from the world, but most of the orders deploy lay servants for the world. The Jesuits are the largest, over 19,000 strong; with both priests and brothers in the order, they have introduced higher education into 37 countries. In her lifetime, Mother Teresa brought enormous visibility to the Missionaries of Charity, which she started in 1950; today, the order's 4,500 sisters serve homeless, unwanted, critically ill, and dying people in 133 countries. Opus Dei is now the most famous order in pop culture—largely from Dan Brown's dubious presentation of their work in *The Da Vinci Code*.

So, for almost a thousand years, and largely through several thousand mission orders, Roman Catholic laypeople have found ways around institutionalism to follow Christ and serve people in the world. Other traditions, such as Eastern Orthodoxy and the Anglican Church, also have lay ministry orders.

The Role of Laypersons in the World

Christianity's history actually features many laypersons, groups, and movements as lay specialists in Christian vocation. Many non-ordained people, Catholic and Protestant, were pioneers and game changers in their time. Theological contributors, like Tertullian, Calvin, Kierkegaard, Dante, Milton, Coleridge, Bunyan, G. K. Chesterton, Jacques Maritain, C. S. Lewis, Dorothy Sayers, and Chuck Colson come to mind. It would be impossible to exaggerate the contribution of lay artists to Christian devotion: Leonardo, Michelangelo, and Rembrandt are but three of the legion of artists who have visually dramatized the faith for the peoples. The names of the illustrators who enriched *The Book of Kells* and the names behind splendid Christian architecture, frescoes, and stained glass windows are lost to most of us. More of the names of lay contributors to Christian music, however, come readily to mind. No one can even imagine the number of laity who have made differences in their local communities, whose names are featured in no history book, but are among the faith's heroes.

Laypeople in Christian history, like Count Zinzendorf, have led church reform efforts. Some, like William Wilberforce and Cesar Chavez, led social reform movements. Many Christians have advanced justice and peace through politics and diplomacy. Florence Nightingale advanced the delivery of medical attention and compassion to wounded soldiers, and she advanced the vocation of nursing. Some Christian laypeople, like Joan of Arc, became iconic figures. William Carey, a Baptist layman from Scotland, catalyzed the modern Protestant missionary movement. William Cameron Townsend organized the movement to translate the Bible into every tongue on earth. David Livingstone pioneered in sub-Sahara Africa, and contributed to New Testament scholarship. Dwight L. Moody, John R. Mott, and Bill Bright led movements in evangelization.

Most of the greatest Christian movements were lay-driven. The Celtic Christian movement was essentially a lay Christian movement that reached many of the peoples of what are now Ireland, Scotland, England, and much of western Europe. Eighteenth-century British Methodism was a reproductive unstoppable movement largely because most of the ministry, within the Methodist societies and beyond, was entrusted to the laity. (In time, however, Methodism got over it and became as clergy-dominated as any other tradition.) Since the mid 1960s, after Mao Tse Tung expelled the missionaries and defrocked the indigenous clergy, Chinese Christianity has grown from about four million to over seventy-five million as a lay movement.

The Vision of Hendrik Kraemer

What would it take for Christian lay movements to arise in North America and Europe in the twenty-first century? How would such movements be grounded? What would they look like? What would be some of their distinctive features?

The most notable book on this subject was written over fifty years ago. Hendrik Kraemer's *A Theology of the Laity* was written to address such questions in the European context of that period.[3] He believed that "the relentless secularization of modern life" now made imperative "the resurrected missionary sense of the Church."[4] His historical and theological reflections are foundational for us today.

Kraemer roots the identity of Christian laity in what it meant to be disciples in the New Testament period. The *koine* Greek term was *laicos*, which in time was "Latinized" to *laicos* and *laos*—which became the term that was adapted into most other languages—such as "laity" in English. In the New Testament, we also find the word *kleros*—from which we derive the word "clergy." This modern usage is deceptive however, because in the New Testament the two terms, *laicos* and *kleros*, refer to the same people. In the New Testament, Kraemer observes, "There is no shimmer of an idea of a defined body called 'clergy.'"[5]

In the New Testament, while *laicos* was used more, both terms simply referred to *all* baptized disciples of Jesus, to all members of the Christian movement, to the whole "household of faith," to the whole "people of God." This understanding prevailed for at least the first three generations. Following the gradual emergence of ordination, however, the meaning of "lay" changed inch-by-inch—to something like its widespread meaning today: "unqualified to speak or judge in various fields of knowledge and science."[6] This meaning now is expressed in a number of different flavors. For instance, those of us who are hobbyist magicians remind ourselves that we perform for "laymen," not for other magicians, who are more savvy to the moves and methods that make effects possible! Outside of magic, the term now usually implies (as in the church) a second-class status.

While Luther perceived the problem, and his reformation professed "the priesthood of all believers," the promised recovery was substantially unfulfilled. Luther's church did largely remove the medieval hierarchy, but his emphasis on the priest's role in faithfully preaching and interpreting scripture, which required extensive academic preparation, had the unintended effect of keeping the laity passive.

Furthermore, Luther saw obstacles to the doctrine's immediate implementation. He perceived that not every baptized Christian was actually a believing committed Christian. He perceived that the people in congregations had been kept in dependency and immaturity for too many generations to quickly become an army. Kraemer observed, more broadly, that church structures have not exactly encouraged "lay initiative," and in any case, lay ministry "depends almost entirely on the willingness of the laity to commit themselves."[7]

Kraemer was discouraged by most of the theological literature that addressed the doctrine of the church. Most of that writing, Catholic and Protestant, focused most on who the clergy are and what the clergy do—in preaching, leading worship, counseling, administering the sacraments, and so on. Indeed, the Protestant understanding slipped some after Luther. The most influential Protestant text on ministry, Richard Baxter's *The Reformed Pastor*,[8] has the ordained pastor doing virtually all of the ministry that matters; Baxter's ideal pastor was Eddie Feigner times ten! There aren't even three other essential players in Baxter's paradigm.

Furthermore, Kraemer observed, when writers on the doctrine of the church did give attention to the laity, the focus was usually upon what the clergy should "let" laypeople do in the church, and for the church, in actual ministry beyond, for example, teaching in the Sunday school, singing in the choir, ushering, committee work, and other ecclesiastical chores. Almost no one was writing about what the church's people are called to be and do in the world. That is the focus of Kraemer's significant contribution.

Hendrik Kraemer's great contribution has been to reframe the identity and mission of the laos, theologically, within his doctrine of the church. The following three points are essential:

1. The biblical revelation is clear that **God's great concern is for the world.** Following the fall of Adam and Eve, much of Scripture features God's search for lost humans who need to be found. In Abraham's descendants, the God of Israel raised up a people to be "a light to the nations," to serve as God's agent to bless all peoples, to extend shalom and salvation to the ends of the earth.

When Israel turned inward and misinterpreted her role as God's chosen people, God's game plan changed; a new team was sent to the field. In Jesus' followers, following his resurrection and the gift of the Holy Spirit, the early church was constituted de facto as a New Israel. Jesus taught, "God so loved the world." (Jesus' references to the sparrow and the lily in the Sermon on the Mount and passages like Colossians 1:15-20 taught that God's love includes all humans and extends to other living creatures and to the whole cosmos.)

2. The biblical revelation is clear that **Christ raised up his church to be his mission in the world.** The risen Christ commissioned the church to go to the whole world to love and serve the peoples, communicate the gospel, and make disciples among all peoples. The Church was to be both an *ecclesia*, the "called out" people of God, and an *apostolate*, the "sent out" people of God. In some extended seasons, the church (or at least a substantial population within the church) has obeyed Jesus' mandate. That is, after all, how Christianity became the largest and most worldwide faith. Christ raised up his one, holy, catholic, and apostolic church to be God's mission in the world.

Kraemer observed, however, that the church is often as introverted as Israel was. Indeed, the public in the West typically perceives the church as a self-centered, self-serving, self-glorifying institution. The church was not supposed to live for itself, but to live as ambassadors for Christ in the world. In most churches most of the time, however, "interest in the world is at best a side-issue. . . . The concern . . . which fills the Bible is not even considered 'normal' Christianity within the West's domesticated churches."[9] So Kraemer contended that the renewal of the church is totally dependent upon the rediscovery and passionate affirmation of its identity and main business as Christ's mission in, and for (but not of) the world.

3. We find Kraemer's most important contribution in his declaration of the laity's primary theater for playing their role in God's drama. **The theater of the *laos* is, simply stated, the world.** At least 99 percent of the good that Christians do in the world is achieved by Christian laypeople who know who they are.

The role of most of the clergy, and most other religious professionals, may well be in the church. This arrangement is analogous to the football coach's primary leadership role in the training room and the locker room and from the bench—leading team meetings, teaching the *x*'s and *o*'s, teaching the game plan for each game, revising the game plan and challenging the players at half-time, sending in plays, and so on; the players, in turn, need to learn the playbook, attend the team meetings, and pay attention in the huddle.

However, learning the playbook, attending the meetings and huddles, and dressing like a football player is not what the game is essentially about. If a fellow does all of that but never plays on the field, and isn't really interested, is he really a football player? Likewise, being a Christian is not primarily about attending church or a group meeting, or even reading the Bible or praying; the purpose of all of that, and more, is to form us for following Jesus Christ in ministry in the world. Kraemer wrote, "As the salt pervades all the waters of the ocean, so this eager, interested concern for the world should pervade the Church in all its manifestations."[10] A faithful Church exits not for itself, but for the world; it is God's instrument in the world, for God's purposes.[11] The church is the people of God in ministry and in mission, in imitation of Christ.

Trends in "Avocational" Lay Ministry and Mission

Since Kraemer wrote *A Theology of the Laity*, at least five very important and hopeful trends have emerged in lay ministry and mission:

1. We have seen promising **innovations in lay ministry** within some of the churches. Some laypeople, of course, have always sung in the choir, taught Sunday school, or worked in church governance. The church assumed for hundreds of years that only ordained people could give pastoral care to other people, but in the last generation, we have seen more and more laity engaging in the pastoral care of church members and (in some cases) to people beyond the church. For instance:

□ Mel Steinbron pioneered the training and deployment of laity in pastoral care ministries at College Hill Presbyterian Church in Cincinnati, Ohio. His books, *Can the Pastor Do It Alone?* (Regal Books, 1987) and *The Lay Driven Church* (Regal Books, 1997), and his organization—Lay Pastor Ministry, Inc.—have informed lay pastoral care in hundreds of churches. Following the PACE acronym, lay pastors are committed to:

> Pray for their people daily,
>
> Be Available as needed,
>
> Contact each person weekly, and
>
> Serve as Encouragers and Examples

☐ Leroy Howe, a scholar in theology, philosophy, and psychology, pioneered lay pastoral care ministries in First Methodist Church, Richardson, Texas. His books, especially *A Pastor in Every Pew* (Judson Press, 2000) and *Comforting the Fearful* (Paulist Press, 2002), have deepened this trend and informed this renaissance in lay ministry in many churches; lay pastoral care is often extended to people beyond the church's membership. Howe's curriculum trains lay caregivers to win people's trust through their

> Empathy,
>
> Authenticity,
>
> Respect,
>
> Hope, and
>
> Affirmation

Howe's curriculum also develops a lay shepherd's skills in

> Connecting with people,
>
> Listening to understand,
>
> Mirroring people's feelings,
>
> Reframing people's issues, and in
>
> Appropriate confrontation through conversation

☐ Stephen Ministries, with Lutheran origins, is now helping churches in many traditions to train and deploy lay ministers. They distinctively train laity to help people who are experiencing grief. They also provide training resources for preparing lay people for caring evangelism. While their curriculum requires months of preparation, their website reports that Stephen-trained people are now in ministry in more than eleven thousand congregations.

2. Such approaches to lay pastoral care illustrate another trend. In addition to their vocation of teaching, nursing, sales, farming, or whatever, **increasing numbers of laypeople have entered a Christian avocation.** The avocation is positioned between the full-time vocation of someone who enters a lay order and the two-to-four hours per week of service required for ushering, teaching a class, or singing in the choir.

We can identify at least three distinctive features of the emerging Christian avocation:

a. A Christian avocation typically requires an advanced commitment, a distinctive experience or skill set, and some specialized knowledge or training.

b. The avocational Christian typically invests eight to twelve hours per week in (say) the church's recovery, hospital, shut-in, prison, or grief ministry.

c. The ministry in which people are avocationally involved typically becomes one way they define themselves and are defined by others. It becomes a feature of their identity, they become known for their ministry, and they will be remembered for their avocation in their funeral and obituary.

3. We have witnessed, in many churches, **the emergence of an entrepreneurial laity.** Over and over, a layperson or a group have experienced a vision for serving in a nonconventional way. They see a population that no one is serving or a need that no one is meeting, and they experience a heart for those people. For example, if no manual is available from denominational headquarters on helping children of divorced parents, or gambling addicts, or the new Samoan expatriate people in their city, they create the ministry from scratch—much like one would start a new business or anything else that hadn't been done before, at least locally.

One early example can be documented in the churches in Florida, Arizona, and California that got in early on "the age wave." Many people were living longer, retiring in warmer climates, and were experiencing a new set of issues. One church in Florida revamped the adult Sunday school to be an outreach arm to new retirees from many northern states. They started a Hoosier Sunday school class, then one for Hawkeyes, one for Buckeyes, one for Michiganders, and so on. Two years later, they had 16 new classes serving about 250 new people; half had no prior church to transfer from.

Win and Charles Arn studied many churches serving seniors. Their books, *Catch the Age Wave* (Beacon Hill Press, 1999), *White Unto Harvest* (Institute for American Church Growth, 2003), and *The New Senior* (Institute for American Church Growth, 2004), have instructed many church leaders. More recently, Charles Arn did the field research to script how a church can begin a new ministry with any target population: *Heartbeat: How to Turn Passion into Ministry* (Xulon Press, 2010).

4. Increasingly, entrepreneurial **laity are pioneering outreach ministries**—new ministries created to serve and engage target populations who are mainly outside the church, who may not be like "good church people." The range of populations now being served through some outreach ministry, at least somewhere, is astonishing.

Study enough churches, and you will find some churches serving deaf people, blind people, housebound people, preliterate people, homeless people, addicted people, foster children, street children, at-risk youth, pregnant and parenting teens, military people and their families, prisoners and their families, ex-prisoners and their families, people with mental disabilities, and many others. Search and you will find adoption, auto-repair, medical, dental, clothing, stress-management, anger-management, weight-loss, English-as-a-second-language, animal-welfare ministries, and an astonishing range of support groups.

You will often find laity taking ministry initiatives in trailer park, apartment, ethnic minority, and refugee communities. You will often find laity facilitating the beginning of Spanish, Creole, Cantonese, or Korean Sunday school classes, fellowships, and congregations.

You will often find that ministry to a target population involves multiple programs and ministries. Outreach to addicted populations, for instance, might involve Alcoholics Anonymous, Narcotics Anonymous, and Gamblers Anonymous twelve-step meetings, as well as counseling services, Adult Children of Alcoholics, Al-Anon, and a recovery congregation. Virtually all such ministries are lay-conceived, lay-planned, lay-led, and lay-executed.

5. Increasingly, **lay people are engaging in avocational outreach ministries in teams**—which is the subject of the next chapter.

MISSIONAL CHRISTIANITY IS A "TEAM GAME"

We are asking whether the leaders of over two hundred thousand churches more or less like Old East Church (and the other underachieving types) can get their "apostolic act" together. The previous chapter identified a formidable barrier to this ever happening: a pathological "paradigm," i.e., the set of assumptions called "the clergy-laity heresy." This paradigm results in the benchwarming status of most of the players on Christianity's teams. We suggested that as churches recover early Christianity's character as a lay movement and as they open the doors for an entrepreneurial laity to proliferate outreach ministries in and for the community, churches can and will regain momentum.

The second deeper cause for Old East Side's stagnation, which we address in this chapter, is the unquestioned *individualism* that pervades Old East Side's culture. In a typical church, most of the ministry that really matters is assigned to the pastor; some other ministries are assigned to individual lay volunteers. So, Larry plays the organ and Louise leads the choir, Marvin visits the hospitals and Martha visits the shut-ins, Sally keeps the books and Sam is the scoutmaster, and so on. (No one does "outreach," because no one feels "comfortable" with it; besides, taking care of "our people" is now the church's priority.) What is widely assumed to be "normal" church life is organized that way; the reining paradigm is Western individualism, embodied and assumed to be Christian. The individualism paradigm is unconscious, entrenched, and never questioned.

From the Beginning

Christianity's long apostolic tradition, stretching back to the Christian movement's first generation, has much to teach Old East Side about being the church in mission. One indispensable lesson is that missional Christianity is a team game. Christianity was never supposed to be analogous to golf, tennis, or weight lifting—sports that people participate in essentially as individuals. Christianity was supposed to be more analogous to basketball or football—in which people participate as a team; they have specific roles in the team's game plan, but the player who makes it about his stats or an ESPN highlight reel undermines the team's goals in a team game.

A team can be defined as a group of people who pull together to achieve something that the same collection of people, as individuals, could never achieve. Good teams become far more than the sum of their parts.

A team approach to local church ministry presupposes what was supposed to be a cardinal doctrine of Reformation Christianity—the Priesthood of all Believers. At least since the seventeenth-century publication of Richard Baxter's *The Reformed Pastor*, however, the doctrine was seldom implemented. In Baxter's model, the pastor is everybody's chaplain; the congregation is an audience, not an army.

The church is Eddie Feigner, with several other people standing around and occasionally assisting.

Scriptures, however, often feature ministry as much more widely shared. A notable example is recorded in the book of Exodus. Early in the forty-year circuitous route that the Israelites took to reach the Promised Land, the people were often dissatisfied, and they "complained against Moses;" Moses was exhausting himself in trying to manage the conflict, counsel the people, settle all disputes, and so on. One day, his father-in-law, Jethro, surfaced as history's first known organizational consultant; he told Moses, "What you are doing isn't good!" Jethro taught Moses how to get ministry done through other people. Ten people would do ministry and report to Moses, and each of those ten would manage ten other people in ministry. And they would learn from each other, and support each other, in this wider ministry. In time, many people were in ministry, serving more people than Moses ever could have served in a Lone Ranger ministry model, and ta-da—Moses had a life again!

The New Testament Gospels model a supremely important principle for outreach in an apostolic context. Jesus called a dozen people to join in company with him in his emerging ministry in Galilee and beyond. They became arguably history's most important team. *As a Team,* Jesus and the disciples engaged in ministry with blind people and deaf people, mentally ill people and possessed people, lepers and prostitutes, tax collectors and zealots, Samaritans and Gentiles, and others—all of them banned from the Temple. Perhaps an individual priest can minister to the Temple "regulars," but it takes a team to engage the populations that establishment religion regards as hopeless.

No one in the earliest Christian movement was ordained in the sense that any Christian tradition now means; and no one was ordained for at least a century. The early Christian movement was a lay movement in which disciples supported each other, learned from each other, interceded for each other, and did ministry to pre-

Christian populations—in teams. The early church was essentially a constellation of house churches in every city where Christianity was planted; house churches were typically led in worship, learning, ministry, and witness by de facto teams of several people. Furthermore, the disciples who became apostles (and also Paul) typically traveled, engaged pre-Christian populations, and planted house churches in one community after another *as* "apostolic bands." (Romans 16 reveals that women were numbered among the apostles; third- and fourth-century writings, such as the Acts of Philip, remember both men and women within the apostolic teams.)

In time, the church substantially lost the vision to reach pre-Christian populations. So the church deployed apostolic teams less and less as the movement ordained priests, built churches for gathered congregations, and settled into what became conventional parish life in the empire's cities. There were fourth-generation exceptions, like the work of Irenaeus and (we think) his team among the Gauls. In time, however, outreach to pagan populations virtually ceased, and the earlier apostolic mission to "barbarian" populations was now assumed to be impossible to achieve. The Goths, the Visigoths, the Franks, the Frisians, the Vandals, the Celtic peoples, and many others were now, by definition, not civilized enough to become "Christianized."

The year 432 AD marks the historic recovery of the tradition of deploying apostolic teams to reach pre-Christian populations. In that year, Patrick led an apostolic team to reach the Irish. Technically, Christianity was probably already present on the island; there were probably several expatriate congregations for Latin-speaking "foreigners." Patrick's team, however, reached inland to a settlement called Saul and stayed long enough to plant the first indigenous church among the Irish people. In time, the team moved on to another settlement to replicate the process.

They did this again and again, for the remaining twenty-eight years of Patrick's life. The team's goal in each settlement was to raise up a core of new believers, disciple and form them into an interdependent team, and entrust the expansion of the new local movement to them before moving on. In time, the young Irish Christian movement established monastic communities—each led by an abbot or abbess, and his or her team. The monastic community immersed its people in the Scriptures, nurtured and empowered them through community worship and small group life, and prepared people after several months or several seasons to form into apostolic teams to reach more pre-Christian settlements. Within a century, a higher percentage of Irish people were serious Christians than any other province within the Roman Empire.

Through apostolic teams led by Columba, Aidan, and Columbanus, the movement reached the Picts of Scotland, and the Anglo-Saxons that now populated England, and many of the "barbarian" peoples of western Europe; they, thereby, evangelized western Europe for a second time, and brought Europe out of the so-called Dark Ages. That, in the words of historian Thomas Cahill, is "how the Irish saved civilization!"

In Christianity's entire history, most (if not all) of the great pioneering missions to new populations have been team achievements. While history may only recall the name of the team leader, a devoted, disciplined team in the Spirit's service planted the faith in each land and among each people, included new indigenous leaders in their company, and deployed them in the work as soon as possible.

*   *   *

Almost as typically, apostolic movements to reach pre-Christian populations in lands where the church has long been present are also team ministries. Eighteenth-century Methodism in the British Isles provides an exemplary case.

Two events pushed and pulled so many people from the countryside that England rapidly became the world's first substantially urban nation. First, what had long-been the common lands, where anyone could farm or graze their livestock, were now privatized, fenced, enclosed; suddenly many people could no longer make a living where they'd been raised. Meanwhile, and second, the new factories in the cities needed workers. So rural people now flooded into London and other industrial cities for jobs. The Church of England, of course, already had churches and geographic parishes in the cities. But those churches did not reach the new urban working poor people, nor (with astonishingly few exceptions) did they even try.

The reason why the churches neglected the city's new citizens remains something of a mystery, and each historian seems to have a favorite explanation, or excuse. Permit me to propose my own theory. The church's leaders and people played and replayed an old tape from a fifteen-hundred-year-old paradigm: they perceived the new people as not "civilized" enough to be "Christianized." If we could hear a recording of the comments of church leaders, we would recognize a familiar pattern: they would have misperceived the changes now taking place in their city as a threat rather than an opportunity, as an old community dying rather than a new community now being born—and yet to be shaped. (Those are the paradigm-level issues behind the demise of most churches in changing communities everywhere, in every age.)

More specifically, we'd hear something like the following: "Look at those people who have moved into our city. They do not dress like we do, or talk like we do, and we hear they have some really tacky habits. They obviously cannot afford to rent a pew; they obviously are not literate enough to navigate the Book of Common Prayer. If they came to church, they would have no idea when to sit, or stand, or kneel; they'd have no idea how to find Second Kings or Second Corinthians. If they actually said anything in our church, they might utter an expletive or even split an infinitive. How could such people ever become good Christians, like us?" From the assumption that this would be impossible—at least until "they" first became "civilized"—the established churches did nothing.

Once again, an apostolic pioneer demonstrated that the impossible was possible. His name was John Wesley. As a boy, he had observed his mother's ministry with "common people" in her kitchen in Epworth. As a young man, he reflected from his experience in ministry in prisons. He reflected from his experience in the "Holy Club" in Oxford—a de facto team in which the members ministered with each other and engaged in spiritual disciplines and outreach ministry together.

In Wesley's mind, the idea of the apostolic team was reborn once again. In Wesley's career, he traveled some 225,000 miles, itinerating from town to town to preach, minister, plant Methodism, and, once planted, to encourage the local leaders. The many artists who have painted John Wesley as traveling alone, a solitary figure on horseback, got that one wrong. For starters, no one traveled alone on England's eighteenth-century "highways." They'd have been open prey for bandits; people traveled in groups. In any case, Wesley traveled with a team; the major exceptions were when the team swelled to an entourage. As they traveled, Wesley did contextual training, and they reported and reflected upon what they had experienced in ministry in the town they just left; some of this insight found its way into Wesley's Journal.

In each town, as a crowd gathered for the open-air meeting where Wesley would speak, team members scattered among the crowd and engaged receptive people in the ministry of conversation. The goal of an open-air meeting was to enroll receptive people in a de facto team experience called a class meeting, in which the people engaged in ministry with each other in the mutual commitment to live new lives. People wanting still more discipline formed into bands. The class meetings, together, constituted a Methodist Society—with Sunday evening worship. A team of stewards governed the Society. Other teams formed to teach children, or visit from house to house, or visit the hospital, or engage in a range of other ministries. Early Methodism grew substantially as a team-based lay-Christian movement.

The Rediscovery of Teams

In the last generation or so, the wisdom of teams for all kinds of organization has been widely rediscovered. Two decades ago, Warren Bennis did extensive field research and reconceived the theory of leadership. His conclusions were published in *Leaders: The Strategies of Taking Charge* and in two succeeding volumes.[1] His project was universally admired, and his insights are perennially useful—with one exception.

In book reviews, Bennis' colleagues identified one enormous omission. He was still functioning within the "great man" leadership paradigm. His colleagues pointed out that the single top leader paradigm is no longer viable for one simple reason: knowledge has become so unmanageably vast that the effective leadership of organizations is becoming increasingly interdisciplinary; no one leader now knows enough to provide Lone Ranger leadership.

So the *effective* top leader now gathers a team of people who know far more in their knowledge area than the leader could possibly know, and each team member is essentially the leader in their area; the team makes decisions and plans for the future collaboratively, tapping into the wider knowledge base that the team makes possible.[2]

Much of the twentieth century's most notable achievements was accomplished by teams, and not without them. In 1990, I toured the Marshall Space Flight Center in Huntsville, Alabama. My tour guide, a layman in the local Methodist church, had served with Werner Von Braun on the team that developed the Saturn V rocket that propelled the Apollo spaceship and its crew to the moon in 1969. I asked him to reflect on that experience. The following comment is nearly verbatim: "Dr. Von Braun was a great rocket scientist, and he was so secure in his brilliance that he knew he could not design and build the rocket by himself. He selected people who, in specific areas, knew much more than he did; then he trusted us, and he campaigned for the funding, and he believed in us, and he loved us, and we loved him and each other, and he convinced us that we could achieve something unprecedented." Then my host added, "It was the most wonderful time of my life. I have missed that time, and Dr. Von Braun, and all the guys, ever since."

I have interviewed many men who report that their military service was the most profound and meaningful experience in their lives. In the face of a common threat, in their life together in the trenches, in pulling together to achieve each mission, and in the shared experience of wounds or the loss of buddies, they experienced greater love, closeness, and solidarity with others than they once knew was possible. Decades later, they look back upon that time as the peak experience of their lives.

Athletic teams occasionally experience such bonding. In the 1957–58 school year, Ed Beck was the center and captain of the University of Kentucky's basketball team. Ed's wife was critically ill and died in 1957. The whole team became like brothers. Although they were not the most athletically talented squad in the nation, with a half-dozen season losses, they came together with emotional power and won the 1958 NCAA championship. From that notable experience, Beck, Vernon Hatton, Johnny Cox and the others have been like brothers for life. Ed's later book, *A Love to Live By*, tells the story (Here's Life Publishers, 1984). Ed and I became close friends in divinity school. Later, I served on the staff that he led for the Methodist Church's Board of Evangelism, and I tasted the meaning of life in a serious team. From that experience, I was able to lead two teams—a staff at a denominational agency and a faculty at a large divinity school.

I have often thought that this may be the major missing ingredient with men in the ministry of most local churches. Pragmatically, church leaders have found that it is enormously easier to recruit men to join a "team" than to join a "small group." A team is, of course, a type of small group, but sometimes it matters what you call it! (No bait and switch is involved. Recruiters explain up front, "We huddle, like other teams.") If we started challenging and recruiting men to do great things in Christ's service and formed and mobilized them in groups that became teams, we would discover that such experience can transcend what even sport or war can offer in relational meaning.

I once learned, the hard way, how nearly indispensable a team approach to outreach ministry must be. I spent the summer of 1962, while in divinity school, in outreach ministry to the people of "Muscle Beach" in Southern California. The setting was challenging. I was in ministry to the muscle crowd, to beatniks, homosexuals, surfers, and several other groups. Virtually all of them had one thing in common. Most of them had no Christian memory, no church to one day "return" to; they had no prior knowledge of what I was talking about. They were really secular people!

That summer, some became Christians, more became open to faith, and many experienced helpful ministry in part because I was there. God used the experience to rub my face in secularity; I discovered some questions and issues I have worked with ever since in the quest to help churches understand, serve, and reach secular people. That summer, however, every day for three months, I walked to the beach *alone*, and spent the day at the beach in conversation with people, morning, afternoon, and evening, for three months, *alone*. Did I mention that I always did this "*alone?*" Later in my studies, when I discovered that apostolic ministry is usually done by and through apostolic teams, a blinding flash of the obvious assaulted me; it made total sense.

Today, the churches that are indeed serving and reaching pre-Christian populations are usually doing it through teams. If an indigenous worship service is engaging pre-Christian seekers, the service is likely planned and delivered by a worship team. If the church is keeping its youth and reaching unchurched youth, the youth ministry probably emerges from the devotion and planning of a team of adults and youth. If a church is reaching alcoholics and other addicts, behind it you will likely find a team of compassionate no-nonsense leaders who are themselves in recovery.

More widely, the dominant trend in new church planting involves church planting teams; the Lone Ranger church planter is almost an endangered species. And if the church has a serious involvement in world mission, then, in addition to supporting missionaries (usually missionary teams), it typically deploys teams of laity in short-term mission experiences, in which, for example, for three weeks they dig wells or put a roof on a chapel or serve in a dental clinic in a village in India or Guatemala, while gathering each evening in worship and fellowship with indigenous believers. As Pastor Bruce Larson used to say, in those three weeks "they do no harm, they do a little good, they discover who they are, and they come back home on fire for mission."

If Old East Side Church really wants to get its act together, move from decline to growth, and make a difference in people's lives and in the life of the community, it will happen through teams. Many of the accounts of churches that have experienced turnarounds in recent history reveal this unmistakably. For instance, when Don Morgan became pastor of First Church of Christ (a United Church of Christ congregation) in Wethersfield, Connecticut, the church's membership had declined for many years. By the time Morgan retired, the church had more than three thousand members. Morgan tells the story in *Share the Dream, Build the Team* (Baker Books, 2001).

On Becoming a Team-Based Local Movement

So how does Old East Side become a team-based local movement? It does *not* happen the way that many church leaders typically respond: by adopting the jargon. I have studied many churches whose leaders were now saying, "We are a missional church," but not much had actually changed. Saying that a group is a team does not make it a team. To *become* a team, the group would necessarily go through a studied process that behavioral scientists call "team building." I am resisting the temptation to summarize that process for the reader because no one understands enough from a *Reader's Digest* condensed version to make it happen.

As a preview, I can predict that the process would go through several stages—that scholars have named Forming, Storming, Norming, and Performing. And I can profile what a group looks like after becoming a team:

1. The team has a clear mission that contributes to the organization's mission.

2. Each team member is needed because he or she contributes essential knowledge or skills.

3. While the team exists primarily for its mission, team members support each other socio-emotionally.

4. Each member has an essential role in the team's success.

5. Leadership is much more shared than in typical groups or traditional organizations.

6. The team's members hold themselves in voluntary accountability to each other.

7. Effective teams spend much more *time* with each other than typical groups. Time spent together is essential to the great rapport and interdependency that characterize great teams.

8. Every team member is on the same page, but not at the same place on that page. If everyone thinks alike, or is expected to think alike, that breeds "GroupThink"—the conformity-pathology to which close groups are vulnerable.

Recruiting Laypeople for Ministries: Three Models

We are not featuring the Team Ministry model because it is an exciting new thing to try for a while, but because it is the predominant perennial model for the people of God engaging in outreach ministries to pre-Christian target populations, and because it is needed now even more than it was in less complex times. The future of effective Christian outreach involves teams of committed laity, often entrepreneurial laity, who have affirmed a Christian avocation and are living out that avocation together.

The initial challenge, of course, is to recruit players for the game who have been riding the bench for a long time. Many of our dutiful attenders have never been invited, much less challenged, to do anything for Christ in the world. At least three basic models have impressive track records.

One, pioneered by John Ed Mathison and his people at Frazer Memorial United Methodist Church in Montgomery, Alabama, involves the scheduled, systematic, public invitation for people to volunteer in a specific ministry for a year. The title of Mathison's book, *Every Member in Ministry* (Discipleship Resources, 1992), suggests that a major change in a local church's culture is involved—from the people as attenders to the people in ministry. In October and November of each year, the church features a menu of ministry options with the bulletin and in mailings; the menu names and describes over one hundred ministry options—followed by a blank space in which people can describe a new ministry they'd like to help start. People sign up in December, are trained in January, and then serve in that ministry team from February through the next January. For many years, over 90 percent of Frazer's members have been involved in some ministry.

A second recruitment model begins by helping people discover greater insight into how they are gifted for ministry. The model is based on Pentecostal Christianity's contribution to the whole church—the doctrine that the Holy Spirit has entrusted to every believer one or more spiritual gifts for ministry in, and beyond, the Body of Christ. The Houts Spiritual Gifts Inventory has been widely used for this purpose for several decades. When people fill in the questionnaire, they respond to over one hundred statements by recording the degree to which (much, some, little, never) each statement reflects who they *are* (not who they wish to be). The Houts Inventory can now be accessed online, and a number of leaders, including C. Peter Wagner,[3] have published versions of such an inventory. (The effect of discovering one's gifts is usually more reinforcing than revelatory; for instance, I have never met anyone who discovered the spiritual gift for hospitality who hadn't kind of known that already.)

Third, Rick Warren, founding pastor of Saddleback Church in Southern California, faced the challenge of "turning an audience into an army" by helping people discover their "SHAPE." As explained in *The Purpose Driven Church* (Zondervan, 1995), Saddleback's people take a four-hour Sunday afternoon self-assessment seminar[4] in which they discover their:

> **S**piritual Gifts
>
> **H**eart (what they have a passion for)
>
> **A**bilities (what they are best at)
>
> **P**ersonality Type (from a version of the Myers-Briggs inventory)
>
> **E**xperiences (life, educational, vocational, and painful experiences)

People take with them a personalized document showing their assessment results. They check the accuracy of their responses with the people who know them best. The next Sunday afternoon, with their revised instrument in hand, they meet with a lay counselor whose ministry is to help other laypeople find their ministry. They identify the two or three of Saddleback's more-than one hundred ministries for which they are most obviously shaped. They choose one of the salient options, and soon they are in ministry.

Initiating New Outreach Ministries

A great many churches now feature more than twenty-five lay ministries; many churches feature more than fifty; you don't have to look too far to find a church with more than one hundred.

Most of the ministries were conceived in the imagination of one or more entrepreneurial laypeople who saw a need in the community. For example, they perceived some single moms needing a support group or a weekly mother's day out; or they perceived some expatriate families who needed to learn English or gather in a Filipino fellowship; or they perceived some overweight people with health and self-esteem issues.

While every opportunity to serve is at least somewhat unique, the path to most new ministries will take the following steps:

1. Identify an underserved target population within your community.

2. Discover if enough of you have a "heart" for the population to enable a ministry to fly.

3. Read. Learn what you can about people like them from books, articles, and the Internet. (But be discriminating; not all Internet sources are created equal!)

4. Network with others who understand them, work with them, cross bridges to them. Build alliances.

5. From steps three and four, cogently "profile" the target population. Distill your "intelligence" into something like a six-page document of insights that will inform your planning; revise that profile as you learn more, and as the population or situation change.

6. Get really serious, and move the ministry's development to the front burner, when you have more than enough leaders—with the heart and the knowledge and skills you need or eagerness to learn.

7. Do not begin from scratch unless you have to—do not reinvent any wheel unless you have to. Stand on the shoulders of churches and local Christian movements that are already doing some version of what you are called to do. Do some field research in those churches; study those ministries. Interview some of the people who have been reached and helped by this ministry, so you can tell their story back home. Ask the ministry's leaders questions similar to the following:[5]

   a. Who is this ministry serving? What are the distinctive features and needs you have discovered in this target population?

   b. What is the context of this ministry?

   c. What is the history of this ministry?

   d. What are the specific programs of this ministry?

   e. How is this ministry organized?

   f. What are the costs of this ministry—in human resources and physical resources?

   g. What is the explicit and implied theology informing this ministry?

   h. What kinds of knowledge and skills are necessary in this ministry?

    i. What people, churches, literature, and sources have been the most important in informing this ministry?

    j. What does this ministry do well?

    k. What does this ministry leave undone?

    l. What are the future possibilities for this ministry?

    m. Knowing what you know now, what would you do differently if you were starting this ministry today?

8. Manage the ministry collaboratively, following all of the essential steps involved in "getting things done through other people."[6]

    a. Situation Analysis ("Where are we now?")

    b. Planning ("Where do we want to go?")

    c. Human Resources ("Who do we need to get us there?")

    d. Physical Resources ("What will they need to get us there?")

    e. Performance Standards ("How well should our people do their work?")

    f. Performance Appraisal ("How well are they doing their work?")

    g. Development and Controls ("How can we help them do better?")

    h. Incentives and Rewards ("How can we affirm work well done?")

9. Activate your networks, advertise the new ministry, get the word out, and invite, invite, and invite.

10. Continually make explicit, record, and rehearse what you are learning.

11. Periodically evaluate the ministry and make strategic adjustments.

12. In the church, bathe the outreach ministries in prayer, reinforce the outreach movement's driving values in the life of the church, tell the stories of God's grace, **because the outreach ministry of the laity in the world is the main business of the church.**

The Ministry of Evangelism within Outreach Ministry

The biggest mistake that churches make in mission, whether at home or overseas, is serving people—often in many different ways, without helping them to become followers of Christ. You would not have to search very long or far, in about any nation in Asia, Africa, or Latin America, to find a mission station whose personnel are teaching literacy to adults, educating children, filling teeth, giving inoculations, digging wells, and serving in still other ways, but never getting around to doing the one thing for which the risen Christ explicitly mandated his people to do: go, communicate the gospel, and make disciples among all peoples.

Doing mission without doing evangelism typically has unfortunate unintended consequences. It may perpetuate dependency. It may perpetuate the chief mistake of the colonialism era: despite its good intentions and noble ministries, the people experience the mission to be paternalistic. It may lead the people to conclude that we want to serve them but that we do not want them, and God may not either. If we serve people in all the ways that we can think of, but neglect to help them experience forgiveness, justification, second birth, new life, and God's purpose for their lives, we will leave them ultimately impoverished.

An outreach ministry actually provides the credibility and opportunity to reach people that evangelism alone could never reach. That is understandable, because people are more than souls with ears. There is one practical stipulation: we are called to do evangelism in ways that are congruent with the outreach ministry. Consider the following guidelines:

1. **Connect** with the new people you are beginning to serve. You want friendships to emerge, relationships to develop, trust to replace any initial suspicion.

2. Get in **conversation** with the people you are serving. As soon as possible, include God in the conversation.

3. **Communicate**, early and often, some of the indispensable Christian truths and stories from the Scriptures. Some of these texts may be specific to their issues; some are God's basic good news intended for all people.

4. **Consign** them, before they believe, to start helping in the ministry and to invite their peers to the ministry.

5. Involve the people in the wider life of the **community** of Faith. After all, the faith is more caught than taught. There's no point in isolating people to the outreach ministry that is helping them.

6. When they believe, ask them to **commit** to Jesus Christ as Lord, to the ministry, and to the church.

7. Ground them in **catechesis**. For centuries, this has included helping people learn the Ten Commandments, the Lord's Prayer, and the Apostle's Creed—by heart. Some churches ground new believers in the Sermon on the Mount, because secular postmodern new people want to know how to live their lives.

8. **Commend** them for roles, including leadership roles, in the ministry—consistent with their SHAPE and into Christian conversation with pre-Christian peers.

Chapter Four

WHO (OR WHAT) WILL WE LEARN FROM?

Have you ever noticed that many people seem to be *very* selective about who (and what) they are willing to learn from? For example, many Democrats and Republicans assume they have nothing to learn from the other party. Many church members assume there's really nothing to learn from theologians. Some theologians assume that psychologists, sociologists, and anthropologists have no insights that theologians need to know; reciprocally, many behavioral scientists cannot even name a single living theologian! Some Americans assume that we have absolutely nothing to learn from Europe; other Americans, however, seem to buy *any* idea made in Europe.

In the world of ideas, most people consider the source. People are more likely to open their minds to sources they identify with or trust and to ideas they already agree with (selective exposure). People are more likely to pay attention to sources they trust and ideas they already affirm (selective attention). People remember reinforcing messages better than new ideas or information (selective recall). Indeed, many people will agree with practically anything that a highly favored source says; consider how many people are influenced by their favorite celebrity.

Folk wisdom and favored sources often drive beliefs, values, and decisions in sports as well. A splendid 2011 film, *Moneyball*, based on a true story, dramatizes this point. A good Oakland Athletics baseball team, following the 2002 season, lost their best players to other teams with bigger payrolls. General Manager Billy Beane (played by Brad Pitt) was faced with the challenge of replacing such players within the budget constraints of his small market team. To the astonishment of the A's organization, Beane hired a young Yale economics graduate, Peter Brand, to be his assistant general manager.

Brand introduced an unprecedented "sabermetrics" approach to scouting and appraising baseball players. The A's staff of scouts stiffly opposed Brand and his methods. After all, they'd never heard of him, he wasn't even "a baseball man," and his views were different from what baseball scouts had learned from many years of accumulated wisdom. We've never done it this way before! What could an Ivy League geek possibly teach experienced major league baseball scouts?

Peter Brand, with Beane's support, patiently explained his perspective with insights such as this one: the scouts had been searching for players with batting averages as high as the players they lost. However, most players with batting averages that good will sign with teams that can pay them more.

Brand proposed that the A's pay serious attention, instead, to each prospect's "on-base percentage." After all, it doesn't matter *how* a batter gets on base—hit, walk, hit-by-pitch, or fielding error. He bought some plausibility with this one insight: the A's cannot afford a team with the batting averages they have traditionally valued, but the A's *can* afford a team of players who get on base as often!

With the new recruitment game plan in place, Beane and Brand assembled a substantially new team. After many losses early in the season and an avalanche of criticism, the team jelled, won a league record of twenty consecutive games, and won their division before losing to the Minnesota Twins in the playoffs. The word was out. The Boston Red Sox offered Beane the moon to become their GM; he declined, but Beane and Brand briefed the Red Sox on the sabermetrics approach. Two years later, the Boston Red Sox won the World Series, their first since 1918.

The leaders of most baseball teams—high school, college, minor league, and major league—have since revised the kind of intelligence that informs player recruitment and selection, and some teams have won championships by adopting this innovation earlier than their competitors.

Can Church Leaders Overcome a "Learning Disability"?

However, demonstrably effective innovations do not sweep across the culture of church leaders as rapidly as in the coaching profession. Most church leaders resemble the A's scouting staff before Peter Brand's arrival; they navigate their churches by the traditional wisdom that served the churches adequately in Christendom and in more recent settled times. In the face of innovations, "We've never done it that way before" has become as automatic as any liturgical response. Today, however, "The rusty swords of the old world are powerless to combat the evils of today and tomorrow" (Dietrich Bonhoeffer). And, the merely trendy and the merely politically correct approaches are as impotent.

To frame it another way, most churches—whether they are driven by the traditionalism agenda, the diversity agenda, or the contemporary agenda, are not "learning organizations." I

79

realize that the suggestion that many "contemporary" churches aren't really learning much any more may strike the reader as surprising, but the prevailing paradigm in most "contemporary" churches is rooted in the 1970s. They may still feature new songs or film clips, but Western culture and the community around the church has changed much more than most of the "contemporary" churches have changed. Generally, the more contemporary churches still retain younger church members more than the traditional or diversity churches (and they often receive younger people by transfer from one of those churches), but without a substantial change in their game plan, they will one day be as antediluvian as the old Sunday evening service.

Once upon a time, you gained your "learning" in your college or professional education. When you graduated, that learning served for your entire career—with some reading to keep up to date. However, in a time when communities, societies, markets, populations, and cultures change more rapidly and more unpredictably than our forbears could have even imagined, continuous learning has become the new cost of effectiveness for all organizations—from companies, to universities, to governments, to organizations in the nonprofit and volunteer sectors, including churches. Peter Senge's book *The Fifth Discipline: The Art and Practice of the Learning Organization* (New York: Doubleday, rev. ed. 2006) popularized the "learning organization" term in the mid-1990s; it became the manual that helped many leaders and their people to shift paradigms. Senge observed that many organizations, even some led by very competent people, had a "learning disability."

This chapter will not attempt to summarize Senge's contribution. Some of his emphases, such as the importance of shared vision and team learning are consistent with themes in this book. For insights into themes like systems thinking, mental models, and the organization valuing each member's personal mastery, one should read Senge. However, this chapter faces a more elementary question: Who (and what) are church leaders willing to learn from? Too many church leaders seem to restrict their sources much more than would *any* serious learning organization. Since churches are unique organizations in many ways, I need to ask five questions:

1. Will We Learn from Scripture?

One of the biggest surprises of my career was the discovery that an affirmative answer to this question cannot be assumed; most church leaders do not "do church" in serious conversation with the Scriptures. The reason is ludicrously simple: almost everyone today, across the theological spectrum, assumes that they already know what the Bible teaches, and they assume that however they "do church" is the biblical way! While many people still study the Scriptures for devotional purposes or to ratify what they already believe or to prepare next week's sermon or lesson, studying the Bible for new insight—theological or strategic—is not standard procedure.

So I have spent half a career commending the possibility that the Bible is an enormously greater source of *new* (to us) theological and strategic insight than most church leaders have ever dreamed. People often respond to the example of Roland Allen. Allen was a late nineteenth-century Anglican missionary to China when illness forced him to return home to England. The more he reflected on his missionary experience, the more he perceived the need to recover a more biblical approach to expressing Christianity's mission. He published a study of St. Paul's missionary methods that were perennial and vastly superior, in strategic insight, to the approaches of the mission agencies and societies of his time. *Missionary Methods: St. Paul's Or Ours?* (RealClassic. com, 2012) experienced a revolutionary and enduring impact.

Let me illustrate the church's problem with two recent examples from my own modest contributions to published biblical study. In some field teaching and then in *Radical Outreach* (Abingdon, 2003, chap. 7), I reflected from the account in John 4 of Jesus' ministry with a Samaritan woman. The passage has much to teach church leaders about secular people who are not like "good church people," and it provides guidelines for reaching them. In more recent field teaching, and then in *The Apostolic Congregation* (Abingdon, 2000, chap. 6), I taught and dramatized some of what is involved in helping people experience initial faith by drawing from the Book of Ruth as our earliest available case study. In response to both lessons, most of the people who said anything expressed surprise that new insight for ministry was available from those passages; they had assumed that their church's conventional preaching and teaching had already milked such passages for about all that they could ever teach us.

2. Will We Learn from Our Tradition?

In addition to simply taking their scriptural knowledge for granted, the leaders of most stagnant and declining churches are at least as oblivious to the strategic wisdom of the Christian tradition and to the founding genius of their church's denominational tradition. Again, the main reason is ludicrously simple. Each tradition has had at least one generation of denominational leaders who were endowed with more hubris and testosterone than good sense, who agreed among themselves that they knew more and they knew better than the tradition's early leaders who once reformed a wing of the church, planted churches far and wide, reached new populations, and pioneered missions in other lands. As a consequence, there is more half-buried gold available from the Christian tradition, and from the distinct denominational traditions, than most church leaders have ever imagined.

For an example, I need to reach no further than my own Methodist tradition. Methodists usually know that John Wesley and other early Methodist apostles spoke for the Christian faith in the open air, but they do not know why. They often know that early Methodists met weekly in "class meetings" but have largely forgotten why— other than a tepid appreciation of "small groups." They may know that most of the early Methodist pastors were lay-pastors, and that ordinary Methodist laypeople did most of the ministry, while now expressing the misguided satisfaction that we have since become much more generically Protestant. Furthermore, Wesley and early

Methodism were formed and informed by a cluster of powerful theological themes now largely forgotten; today, it would be hard to find a more severe case of amnesia inhabiting the pews of any denomination in the solar system.

3. Will We Learn from Secular Academic Fields?

We are experiencing a knowledge explosion. There are now more fields of knowledge than anyone can be conversant with. Once upon a time, our forbears studied everything—science, philosophy, history, literature, and more. Those who seemed to have mastered all fields of learning were called renaissance men.

Today, there may be no more renaissance men—of either gender. The sciences have proliferated to include expanded agendas in mathematics, physics, chemistry, astronomy, botany, and zoology and also many more specific fields like medical science, evolutionary biology, astrophysics, and neuroscience. The behavioral (or social) sciences now include such fields as psychology, sociology, anthropology, linguistics, archaeology, economics, geography, and history. More specific, hyphenated, interdisciplinary, and applied fields have emerged, like social psychology, communication, criminology, education, law, government, and the study of leadership and management.

The knowledge explosion raises an essential question: Should Christian leaders, grounded in Scripture and theology, also study other fields of learning? While it is a complex question—a Christian leader's response to astronomy might not be the same as to psychology—80 percent of Christian leaders seem to stand in one of two orientations.

Some Christian leaders seem to trust secular fields more than they trust insight from Christian Scripture, tradition, and thought, or at least if there is a conflict between the two perspectives, secular learning trumps. So if Freud disagreed with Augustine or Luther, Freud was probably right! I remember when transactional analysis became fashionable in the 1970s. For some of the church leaders who bought in, the Christian doctrine of sin was now dispensable because, after all, TA gurus taught, "I'm OK and you're OK," and everybody is OK!

By contrast, some Christian leaders view most nonecclesial learning with distrust. Knowing grammar is okay—to communicate acceptably. (By that reasoning, knowing rhetoric should be okay—to communicate effectively.) But apart from such controlled exceptions, some Christian leaders contend that one only needs to know Scripture, church history, and theology to teach, preach, counsel, and lead churches; some assert that one really only needs to know the Bible. Christians, they say, have no business studying psychology, sociology, anthropology, and other secular fields. This response is not without a history of provocation; some of the early leaders in such fields were public opponents of Christianity.

The problem is that Christian leaders are already behavioral scientists, whether they have read in those fields or not. I have asked over a thousand Christian leaders colloquial questions such as, "What makes people tick? How do people change? What makes the world go 'round?" Almost every Christian leader has articulate and confident answers to such questions; they are behavioral scientists, but often they are *bad* behavioral scientists! (One reason that we study several behavioral sciences in the study of Christian mission is to replace bad behavioral science with better.)

Moreover, an interdisciplinary knowledge base makes us better theologians and interpreters of scripture. For example, one is more likely to understand the dysfunctional family dynamics in the relationship between Joseph and his brothers if one is familiar with some of the literature about dysfunctional families. One is more likely to perceive the power of Jethro's counsel to Moses if one is literate in the lore of management. And no theological writer on the doctrine of human nature has written an influential text in more than a half-century who was not conversant with the views of philosophers and behavioral scientists.

4. Will We Learn from Statistical Data?

The most effective leaders in the major sports all take statistical data seriously. Baseball's obsession with batting averages and earned run averages and so on is legendary. Executives and coaches in the major sports know that a specific datum is only an indicator, that subjective factors are also involved in appraising athletes. But if in football, one wide receiver runs a 10.0 in the 100 meters and another runs 10.5, the coach knows which receiver is more likely to get open to catch a pass and to gain more yardage after the catch. Furthermore, coaches know that data trends are important to monitor; if a thirty-five-year-old third baseman's batting average was .280 for the first ten years of his career, but only .240 in the last two years, knowledge of that data might influence the team's decision about the length of a new contract.

Medical science takes statistical data seriously. The physician visiting a patient in the hospital checks the patient's vital signs—temperature, pulse rate, and blood pressure. Such data are indispensable for inferring what might be happening in the patient. If the patient's blood pressure was 150/100 yesterday and is 180/130 today, the physician starts reflecting upon the range of available medical interventions.

Effective organizations also take the relevant data seriously; struggling organizations often do not. When Lee Iacocca began the 1980s turnaround of Chrysler, he was initially astonished to find what few facts were available to inform his analysis of the company. In his autobiography he recalled, "Even the most rudimentary [financial] questions were impossible for them to answer." They could not even tell him which Chrysler plants had the best and worst return on investment. Bob Waterman was observing twenty-five years ago that the turnaround of an organization typically begins with a search for the facts and a willingness to act on the facts.[1]

The turnaround of churches is likewise dependent upon the facts. Unlike the Chrysler Corporation that Iacocca inherited, struggling churches are not usually foggy about the financial facts. They can show you the church's budget, the pastor's salary, what members gave how much last year, how much goes for mission, and so on.

What church leaders typically ignore are the statistical facts related to ministry!

Some ministry-data are not available because they are not (yet) recorded. The church records some useful data to report to the denomination, such as the official membership and the average worship attendance. But if you ask how many new Christians were received from the world in the last decade (vis-á-vis the children received in the confirmation class), they cannot say. If you ask how many members are involved in small groups (other than Sunday school classes) or how many members are involved in outreach ministries, they cannot say. When I ask why, they usually reply that the denomination does not require them to collect that data. I then suggest that the interests of the denomination's institutional people should not limit the data that local churches use for their local analysis and planning.

If you begin recording that data now, in a year (or less) you will have new clues to how you are doing. Major sports are adding or refining their categories for data all the time. NFL football teams, for instance, have long appraised linebackers based on data like tackles, tackles for loss, and quarterback sacks. In recent years, they have added the category of "hurries."

Often, churches do record important data and then proceed to ignore it. Consider a large-scale example. Grace Reese was an attorney who went to seminary, served churches, and then became a church consultant and writer. With Lily Foundation support, she led a research project to discover *how* mainline denominational churches in the United States reach new people (when they do it). She identified six denominations with similar reporting patterns, with a total of about 30,000 churches. Of those 30,000 churches, they decided to identify the churches that had received at least five new Christians per year for three years; they would research those churches. To their astonishment, only 150 churches met the criteria; one-half of 1 percent.[2] I interviewed several executives in those denominations who had no idea their churches were reaching so few people. Alas, they still seem to be ignoring such data.

5. Will We Learn from Megachurches?

The historically recent phenomenon of the megachurch has emerged as an issue for very many church leaders.[3] In the 1990s, as megachurches proliferated across the landscape (they still do), some Christian leaders thought the megachurch was the obvious wave of the future; churches who didn't aim to be megachurches weren't "visionary," and they "underachieved."

The predictable backlash surfaced with a vengeance. Some leaders of the Emerging Church movement proclaimed that the small fellowship, with no paid leadership, was the obvious wave of the future. Many church leaders assumed an inverse relationship between size and quality; small was better! Most church leaders today seem to prefer churches somewhere between the small and mega-church sizes, but the conclusion that megachurches are unthinkable (and perhaps obscene!) "in our tradition" remains widespread. I recently consulted with twenty church-planting leaders in the new Anglican movement in North America; they assured me, in hallway conversations, that they planned for no megachurches in their movement.

There may be good reasons for a denomination wanting no very large churches (or, for that matter, no very small churches). But the coalitions of church leaders that reach such a policy do not usually offer compelling reasons for their conclusion, nor do they reflect much field-based knowledge of actual megachurches. They have, over time, socially constructed their policy from their peer-group conversations and meetings. Typically, they are surprised to hear that megachurches are not all alike, any more than all small or midsize churches are all alike.

Some leaders of at least several traditional denominations say that they oppose both the very small church model and the very large church model. Most of their churches, however, have experienced net membership decline, and they want their churches to have more people involved than they have today, but the largest size church that is "legitimate" in their paradigm is based on the congregations that their tradition's greatest forbears once preached to in the eighteenth and nineteenth centuries; so four hundred to seven hundred would be very desirable once again.

Meanwhile, Protestant megachurches (defined as churches with 2,000 or more attendees per week), have multiplied across North America in recent history. While there were perhaps 50 such churches in 1970; by 1980 there were about 150; 300 by 1990; 600 by 2000; 1,200 by 2005; and over 1,600 by the end of 2010. But, until recent history, megachurches were virtually without precedent in the experience of most Protestant Christians. Most of our great evangelical predecessors—including Jonathan Edwards and many others—preached to hundreds, not thousands. So when many traditional Protestants are exposed to a megachurch on, for example, one-hundred acres, with 6,000 in weekly attendance, with a staff of eighty, a ten million dollar budget, with traffic reminiscent of a sporting event, and a preacher who may be colorful, interesting, occasionally entertaining, and "does not sound like a preacher"—leaders in other churches often suspect that the megachurch could not possibly be faithful to the evangelical heritage.

The Twin Issues: Possibility and Feasibility

While that *may* be true of a given megachurch (and it may be true of any size church), I have found it useful to view the megachurch phenomenon in a wider framework. For instance, some things are often smaller than our forbears were familiar with; calculators, radios, telephones, and computers come to mind. But some things now are often larger than anything our predecessors could have imagined. Take universities, for instance. Peter Drucker reminded us in *The Age of Discontinuity*, "No university in the Western world had more than 5,000 students before 1914."[4] By 1968, when Drucker's book was published, universities of 20,000 were "medium sized." Today, universities like Ohio State, Arizona State, University of Florida, University of Minnesota (Twin Cities) and the University of Texas (Austin) exceed 50,000 students. Due to factors like the proliferation of academic fields, majors, graduate programs, professional programs, research missions, and the expanding market of prospective students, most of the nation's universities increase in size, year after year, in good economic times and bad. Furthermore, many businesses, hospitals, high schools, shopping malls, stadiums, and other structures, organizations, and institutions have become what our great-grand parents would have regarded as gigantic. We, however, are so used to these larger examples today that we expect them.

The history of the skyscraper presents an interesting analogy to the history of the megachurch. No buildings above 20 stories dominated the skyline of any city before the late nineteenth century; buildings above six stories were rare. Then architects in London, Chicago, and New York City began designing taller and taller buildings. New York City's Chrysler Building was completed in 1930, and the 102-story Empire State Building (1,250 feet, plus the spire) in 1931. In time, Chicago's Sears Tower and New York City's World Trade Center were built taller. Some cities in Latin America and Asia joined the bandwagon. In the late twentieth century, Kuala Lumpur, Malaysia, decided to build the world's tallest building, and then they decided to build two of them! KL's Petronas Twin Towers were the earth's tallest buildings through 2004. Then a taller building was erected in Dubai, United Arab Emirates, and Dubai recently completed a 163-floor skyscraper exceeding 2,700 feet.

Humans have lived in cities for several thousand years. Very tall buildings would have been an obvious solution, centuries ago, to the problem of limited available urban land. For many centuries, however, very tall buildings were not built because they were not possible, for no more profound reason than this: brick or stone walls supported the weight of a building, and our forbears knew the limitations of their load-bearing capacity.

The late nineteenth century innovation of the steel frame, which would serve as a steel skeleton for the walls of future buildings, made much taller buildings possible; indeed, the "sky" seemed to be the limit.

While skyscrapers were now, for the first time possible, they were as yet not feasible—because of the limited number of stairs that most people were willing and able to climb to access the higher floors. If steel framing made skyscrapers possible, the invention of elevators made them feasible. As elevators improved, skyscrapers were built taller, and taller. (Other innovations, like indoor plumbing and air conditioning, contributed.)

*　*　*

The twin issues of possibility and feasibility, illustrated from the history of skyscrapers, provide a perspective for understanding megachurches.

First, the most obvious reason that our forbears did not preach to thousands is that congregations of that size were widely thought to be impossible; for most places, they were indeed improbable, but very large audiences and congregations are not completely without historical precedent. In the eighteenth century, one of the reasons that John Wesley, George Whitefield, and others preached in the open air was because much larger numbers of pre-Christian people could (and would) attend an open-air meeting than could gather into a church; and, if the speaker stood elevated, two thousand or more people could hear in some conditions.

The late nineteenth and early twentieth centuries experienced the rise of occasional megachurches before we knew what to call them. In the late 1800s, Henry Ward Beecher preached to almost 2,000 people twice each Sunday in Plymouth Congregational Church in Brooklyn. Charles Spurgeon's Metropolitan Tabernacle in London, and then Amiee Semple McPherson's Angelus Temple in Los Angeles, permitted the preacher to engage 2,500 or more. These three historic churches, and several others, were considered architectural marvels that made such attendance possible.[5]

Except for the occasional architectural marvel, why were megachurches so rare until recent times? Because the human voice, without amplification, could only reach a congregation of five hundred to seven hundred people. Even that range required that the speaker perform from an elevated pulpit or platform and in an oratorical style of delivery that seems antiquated and pompous to audiences today.

What the steel skeleton did to make much taller buildings possible, the invention and diffusion of the electronic public address system did to make much larger congregations possible. That one technological change—involving a microphone, an amplifier, and loudspeakers (with improvements over time)—rather suddenly made it possible for the human voice to reach thousands. The churches in a few cities quickly perceived the opportunity; in London, in the mid-twentieth century, W. E. Sangster, Leslie Weatherhead, and Donald Soper were preaching to 1,800 or more. In most places, however, the churches ware laboriously slow to infer the significance, to perceive the opportunity, and to take advantage of the new technology. Many churches merely imported a PA system into their existing facility, and essentially the same size congregations could now hear better; larger facilities, to accommodate the much larger congregations that were now possible, emerged little by little. Some pastors, like J. Wallace Hamilton in St. Petersburg, Florida, and then Robert Schuller in Orange County, California, built larger parking lots and preached to people in two thousand or more cars, each parked beside a small speaker that hooked on the driver-side window, like in a drive-in movie theater. It took three decades for many churches to begin building the larger facilities that would take fuller advantage of the electronically amplified voice.

For a while, megachurches were possible but not yet feasible—because of the limited number of people who lived close enough to the church to walk to church. Mass transportation (like subways) made megachurches feasible in some cities (like London), but the innovation that made megachurches feasible almost everywhere was the automobile. The increased ownership of automobiles even made it possible for people to navigate past the neighborhood church, and several other churches, to attend the larger downtown or regional church.

Other innovations contributed to the megachurch's feasibility. The addition of nurseries reduced competition from crying babies. Central heat and air conditioning systems reduced human discomfort and road noise. More recently, the projection of a presenter's face on a large screen has made a simulated conversation with several thousand people possible.

Meanwhile, wider cultural changes influenced people's choices. Society has moved to larger "full-service" schools, supermarkets, malls, and so forth. This trend conditioned many people to expect a range of ministries to help them, and opportunities to serve within a church. Furthermore, it is useful to note that North American Protestant Christianity has no monopoly on large churches. Africa, Asia, and Latin America (combined) have more Protestant megachurches than North America; the four or five largest megachurches are in South Korea. The Roman Catholic Church may have more "mega-parishes" in North America, Europe, Latin America, and sub-Sahara Africa than all Protestant traditions combined.

To sum up, **the main reason we see megachurches dotting the landscape today is that they are now widely possible and feasible.**

Megachurch Facts and Trends

John Vaughan, of www.megachurches.net and the quarterly *Church Growth Today*, frequently publishes updated lists of the one hundred largest churches in North America (and the fifty largest churches in the world). Vaughan reports that about 70 percent of America's largest one hundred churches are in the western or the southern United States. In contrast to the impressions of most church leaders, only about one-third are "independent" churches; the other two-thirds are denominational. (And most of the "independent" churches are in an association or network that looks and functions much like a denomination that is not yet named. ("If it looks like a duck, and walks like a duck, and talks like a duck, it might be a duck!")

I have observed that there are, essentially, two types of megachurches, with contrasting agendas:

1. As the mission of some European Protestant churches was once to make Catholics into Protestants, so some megachurches target members from other churches, and most new members join (de facto) by transfer.[6] So some megachurches are largely filled with younger people who "graduated" from a more traditional church in town.

2. Some other megachurches regard their community as a secular mission field, they target pre-Christian people, and a majority of the people who join those churches have no church to transfer from. (I am commending this second type of megachurch as the type to learn from.)

The mission statement of the Chicago area's Willow Creek Community Church dramatizes this more apostolic agenda: "Our mission is to help irreligious people become fully devoted followers of Jesus Christ." The latter (more apostolic) megachurches, which are driven to reach and disciple populations with no Christian memory, realized that they would have to reinvent the way they "do church" to achieve their mission. The most influential innovations emerged, historically, in the Jesus Movement in the 1970s and 1980s, and in several mega-churches—like Willow Creek and Southern California's Saddleback Church. These bellwether churches influence many other churches through their conferences, publications, and networks—such as the Willow Creek Association (www.willowcreek.com).

* * *

I have observed, however, that many church leaders seriously misread megachurches. They view megachurches through old paradigms, and therefore fail to perceive what they observe! Indeed, what they think they perceive can vary enormously from reality.

For instance, it could be said that when some people notice, for example, the absence of pipe organs and the presence of praise bands, they see "trendy" Christianity or "opposition to tradition"; actually, the church is probably attempting culturally "indigenous" ministry, as effective churches must do on *any* mission field, including ours. Again, people typically see a megachurch on a Sunday morning, without understanding that most megachurches are "seven-day-a-week churches" (Lyle Schaller). Still again, people often identify a megachurch with a specific community and are later astonished at the number of communities it reaches and the range of its global involvement. Often they identify the church with the social class they see attending a specific service and are later astonished by the church's diversity, sometimes including several ethnic-language congregations.

Or, when people see a congregation of several thousand, they attribute the crowd to "great preaching." Actually, most mega-churches put fewer of their eggs in the preaching basket than traditional churches. The preaching is only part of a planned experience. The worship service, whether "seeker sensitive" or "seeker driven," begins where people are, engaging their questions, needs, issues, struggles, and hopes. The service does not presuppose that people have already acquired enough of a "church etiquette" to know what to do and when, so the church adapts the service to make the experience manageable for them.

The service does not presuppose that the target population is adequately informed about the Christian message and lifestyle, so the service may present themes within "Christianity 101." The service's music, drama, video clip, testimony, or a prayer time may be as prominently featured as "the message"; and the message engages an issue in people's lives, from Scripture, in the people's language, in a conversational style. The whole service reflects a more casual, contemporary, culturally relevant, emotionally relevant, celebrative style than one would likely experience in the smaller traditional church down the street that appears stuck in 1956.

When traditional church leaders casually observe a church of thousands, they have no idea that most megachurches "grow larger by growing smaller." The most important feature of many missional megachurches is the small group (sometimes called the "cell group" or the "life group.") Many megachurches involve thousands of people each week in group life—such as neighborhood groups, Bible study groups, nurture groups, support groups, prayer groups, recovery groups, groups for seekers, sports teams, and a great many groups with some ministry beyond the group. Many megachurches are no longer churches "with" small groups; they are "meta-churches" (Carl George) *of* small groups. In meta-churches, many people first join a group and then the church; most people learn, in their small group, to be in ministry with other people, and to converse meaningfully about the faith. So Ralph Neighbor reports that nineteen of the twenty largest churches on earth are "cell churches."

When people learn about a megachurch's large staff, they have no idea that, actually, the church spends about the same percentage of its budget (48 percent) on staff as other churches; mainly, it shepherds and grows its people and attracts seekers and new members through the many ministries of laity. Most of the members are involved in a ministry for which they are gifted, and many of the lay-led ministries are outreach ministries to pre-Christian people. The strongest and most reproductive megachurches are, essentially, local lay movements.

* * *

The 2011 megachurch study published by the Hartford Seminary Foundation (http://hirr.hartsem.edu) has provided additional intelligence about very large churches. The comprehensive study identified 1,611 churches with weekly attendance of over 1,800. They are not as huge as their image would suggest; their average total weekly attendance was 3,597 in 2010. Since a few are very large, the typical megachurch attendance is between 2,000 and 3,000. The median seating capacity in these churches is 1,500; so most megachurches serve their people through two or more worshiping congregations. (The average number of congregations per weekend is 5.5; 5 percent of the megachurches feature 9 or more congregations each weekend.) Most of the churches (nearly 100 percent) schedule one or more services for Sunday morning. Services are often scheduled for Saturday evening (48 percent) or Sunday evening (41 percent); a Saturday or Sunday evening service is often identical to the Sunday morning services. (The strong trend is toward proliferating more and more congregations.) Some features of their worship services do fit their stereotype: 96 percent feature the electric guitar, 97 percent employ visual projection, 98 percent feature percussion instruments; but, contrary to image, 43 percent feature a choir, and 28 percent have an organ.

Alas, the prophesies of the decline and death of megachurches have not materialized. They are growing in number: 1,200+ in 2005, 1,600+ in 2010. They are growing in weekend attendance: 2,600+ in 2005, almost 3,600 in 2010. (That represents 8 percent attendance growth per year for the five years.) Increasingly, these churches welcome people to any one of several congregations on the main campus while also proliferating one-to-several satellite campuses; 46 percent meet and worship in two or more locations. Megachurches require considerably more acreage than traditional churches and, since large tracts of land are no longer available downtown, this necessitates building in a developing section of the city—on a major traffic artery. Some 30 percent of the Hartford survey churches classified themselves as "nondenominational;" 56 percent self-classify as "Evangelical."

Who do they reach? Megachurches are more effective at reaching and involving men; 45 percent of the people who attend are male—a much larger percentage than in most churches. Contrary to their homogeneous image, megachurches are *more* likely to have multi-class, multi-racial, multi-ethnic, multi-lingual, and younger memberships than more traditional churches. Megachurches have adapted to serving in the current recession; over 80 percent have a food pantry and/or a soup kitchen, and they offer financial counseling and cash assistance to people who need it.

Hartford's researchers in their 2005 report did not really surprise us when they explained that megachurches are much larger than other churches because "they attract and retain more persons over time than do other churches." This growth is not primarily due, however, to the megachurch's superior demographic knowledge or marketing savvy; rather, their members are much more energized to invite others, and "megachurches undertake multiple efforts to reach out to nonmembers." Most megachurches are very intentional in responding to visitors and in integrating new people into congregational life—through a mentor, a group, or a lay ministry. Missional megachurches are high-expectation churches; they "demand" more from members than most traditional, contemporary, and diversity churches. Hartford's study tells us that the public rumor that younger people dislike megachurches is unfounded; they reach younger generations virtually as effectively as they once reached Baby Boomers. The Hartford study projects that, in the future, megachurches will continue to proliferate.

Five Indictments against Megachurches

In conclusion, I should add that five charges against mega-churches are substantially true—although that admission, once explained, may grant few debating points to the megachurch's cultured despisers.

One charge is that **megachurches grow by church growth principles**. Since church growth is essentially a *descriptive* discipline, i.e., it's scholars study growing churches and describe the principles that account for their growth, it *should* astonish no one that megachurches grow, broadly, from the same causes as other growing churches worldwide. So your typical apostolic megachurch has grown *because* (in addition to spiritual factors) it identifies and engages receptive populations, invites pre-Christian people across its people's social networks, proliferates groups and lay ministries and congregations, reaches "unlikely" people and thereby catalyzes wider interest, and adapts to its context to do church in culturally and emotionally relevant ways, and so on.[7]

A second charge is also true: that the **leaders of most mega-churches lead by management principles.** The academic field of management, an applied behavioral science once pioneered by Peter Drucker and others, is also a descriptive discipline. The field defines management as "the studied art of getting things done through other people," or "achieving the organization's objectives through other people." By this understanding, most pastors are managers whether they acknowledge it or not.[8] Many pastors are managers, but uninformed and incompetent managers; they typically recruit the wrong people for an office, role, or task, and they play on guilt to get people to say yes, and the people who take the job have no idea what a good job looks like or how the job contributes to the church's mission. My book *Leading and Managing a Growing Church* (Abingdon, 2000) draws from the most authoritative sources to unpack the eight indispensable questions that effective leaders of *all* effective organizations (including churches) need to ask and the ten generic tasks involved in effectively managing any organization, including churches. Lyle Schaller once observed that a lone shepherd is very limited in how many "sheep" he or she can shepherd; church growth requires that the shepherd become a rancher—and learn to get most of the shepherding done through other people.

The third charge against megachurches is that they are thought to do "**marketing**."[9] Detractors often regard this term as the most obscene of the three. The field's most important conceptual pioneer was Philip Kotler, who taught marketing at Northwestern University for many years. He has been the author or coauthor of many influential texts on marketing, including several editions of *Marketing for Nonprofit Organizations.* Kotler has been profoundly interested in how organizations like the Red Cross, relief agencies, universities, hospitals, libraries, theaters, service organizations, and churches most effectively make their services known and available to their "markets," i.e., their target populations. Amazon lists books coauthored by Kotler on the marketing of public leaders, marketing in the public sector, and even the marketing of nations.

The subtitle of one of Kotler's books suggests the case for the church's use: *Marketing for Congregations: Choose to Serve People More Effectively.*[10] I was very influenced by the 1982 edition of his *Marketing for Nonprofit Organizations.* Kotler helped me face what may be the local church's supreme strategic question: "Is a church going to be responsive or unresponsive to the needs of unchurched people in its ministry area?" Reflecting from Kotler, a church's four essential steps in a *responsive* marketing strategy are to: (1) Gather information about the population whom the church believes it is called to reach and serve. (2) Develop ministries that could help them. (3) Communicate the news of the ministry to the target population and invite their involvement. (4) Present the ministry with effectiveness, through the management process.[11] Megachurches that reach people through a range of fifty or more outreach ministries, understandably do follow some version of a strategic marketing process.

The fourth charge, most recently announced from a University of Washington study, is that the **worship at megachurches triggers a "high" in people** that causes them to return for more.[12] These churches, the study claims, present God as "a drug," that the people experience an "oxytocin cocktail of shared transcendent experience." Alas, the writers are kind of on to something, but they lack the academic categories to adequately account for what they observe. What happens in megachurches (and in other inspiring churches) may be more adequately explained in Abraham Maslow's category of "peak experiences."[13]

What may happen in some inspiring worship may be even more adequately explained in the category of sublime experience. A second-century Roman rhetorician, Longinus, reflected upon the powerful aesthetic and emotional experience that great oratory, poetry, music, and drama can stir in people's depth. Much later, Edmund Burke observed that, while Beauty engages the feminine side of our personalities, the Sublime engages the masculine side; deep sublime experiences catalyze the capacity to perceive a matter, and to think about it, differently. Sometimes, he wrote, the sublime experience "anticipates our reasonings, and hurries us on by an irresistible force." Immanuel Kant wrote, "We call that sublime which [we experience as] absolutely great." Sublime experience enables people to respond in deeper thought or commitment. Victor Hugo, Søren Kierkegaard, William Wordsworth, Rudolph Otto, and other notable thinkers have enhanced our understanding of sublime experience.

The University of Washington study seems to suppose that Christianity should be rationally apprehended, only. Christianity, however, is a faith of both the head and the heart. Jonathan Edwards and John Wesley once helped much of Christianity rediscover the importance of "religious affections." Indeed, to become a Christian is, in part, to be delivered from the tyranny of dysfunctional emotions, like fear and anger, into the freedom to experience emotions like gratitude and joy. As Stephen Colbert has reminded us, one reason people go to church is to experience joy. By the narrow view of the University of Washington study, the Hallelujah Chorus of Handel's *Messiah* is suspect![14]

The fifth charge is that **megachurches do not build "depth" in their people**. Actually, some megachurches experience a modest advantage by this criterion. Megachurches that involve their people in small group life, in a range of ministries, and in ministry and witness to pre-Christian people, *as a by-product,* have a somewhat "deeper" membership than the traditional church of pew-sitters down the street. But the difference is only one of degree.

Indeed, it may be impossible to find churches, of any type or size, which build theological depth into even a bare minimal majority of the members. That conclusion is suggestive only, because the criteria for depth are rarely (if ever) defined, and the people who employ the term the most use it to judge growing churches and megachurches with more energy than they judge their own churches! For now, "church depth" is little more than an ecclesiastical slogan!

The concern behind the term, however, has a noble ancestry. Some church leaders, for decades, have been passionately hoping for the church's revival or renewal or internal growth or health or revitalization or formation or depth. Let's admit that, perhaps, *few* churches have got *that* act together yet. Some scholars hypothesize that we are not likely to experience anything like the grounding, strength, life, and depth that we want for our churches without *catechesis, koinonia,* and laity in ministries—and the Holy Spirit's empowerment of the people. But no one knows much of what we need to know about this. One day, some pioneering churches and a great new research tradition will show us the way.

In the meantime, the main conclusion of Willow Creek's *Reveal*[15] study is probably right. There is a limit to how much church programming can do for people. As in adult education, Christians have to take responsibility for their own learning and formation.

* * *

While most churches will not, and should not, become megachurches (any more than most buildings should be skyscrapers), the megachurch is a relatively new, important, and multiplying type of church on North America's religious landscape. Some of them now include more within a church's domain—such as Christian schools, sports leagues, fitness centers, bookstores, and food courts (and much else). With this trend, however, many megachurches may be unwittingly planting the seeds of decline. More Christian kids in church schools means fewer Christian kids in the public schools and fewer Christian parents in the PTA; more Christians pumping iron at church fitness centers means fewer Christians meeting pagans at Gold's Gym. The very churches originally reinvented to reach pre-Christian people, by preparing and sending the laity into the world as salt and light could, over time, become the new evangelical ghettos within the secular city.

For as far as we can anticipate, however, the leaders of some apostolic megachurches will continue to be very important conceptual and strategic pioneers for other church leaders to learn from. You have probably already learned from them. If you feature electronic visual projection on a screen, you got that (directly or indirectly) from a megachurch. If you have a seeker service, or surplus parking, or a Celebrate Recovery program, or new high-energy music, or a second congregation, or a second campus, or a new small group emphasis, or if your people discover their SHAPE and then get into ministry, you probably learned that from a megachurch.

As what we have learned from building skyscrapers now informs how we design and build other buildings, so increasing numbers of church leaders are learning how to do church, ministry, and outreach more effectively from some missional megachurches. Their influence is not limited to North America. Philip Jenkins, whose *God's Continent* [16] is a comprehensive study of Christianity's general decline and challenge in Europe, tells us that most of Europe's notable exceptions (growing churches, in Europe) function much like American megachurches. [17]

Chapter Five

A "SUPPLY SIDE" RESPONSE TO SECULARIZATION EVERYWHERE

Two towering issues confront churches in secular societies and communities. Remarkably, many church leaders ignore these elephants in the room as if they are invisible. The first issue is clearly dramatized in team sports.

Do We "Play to Not Lose" or Do We "Play to Win"?

An NFL football team was winning by almost three touchdowns, when the game's dynamics changed late in the third quarter. Their offense shifted into a more cautious mode—playing to avoid fumbles and interceptions and to consume time on the clock. Three running plays into the line failed to get a first down, so they punted. After a thirty-yard runback, the other team was energized; with nothing now to lose, they played with reckless abandonment, and the home crowd encouragement was now deafening. You guessed it. They scored three touchdowns and won the game. By mid-fourth quarter, the visiting team started running sweeps and passing again, but you could see that they'd lost their "mojo." The TV color commentator observed that the visiting team started out "playing to win;" then they started playing "not to lose;" and momentum, once lost, is hard to regain.

In sports, playing not to lose is sometimes a necessary short-term strategy. So the basketball team, ahead by ten points with ninety seconds left, dribbles and passes and lets each shot clock almost expire before they shoot.

As a longer-term strategy, however, playing not to lose is usually self-defeating. Many churches have experienced this, although their leaders may be in denial. Quite a while ago, they detached from the community and circled the wagons, to protect their people from the influences of a secular community. Since they lost 5 to 7 percent of their members per year, and since detached self-protective churches fail to engage and attract enough replacement members, their membership strength has declined ever since.

The longer cautious churches stay within their comfort zone, the more that zone shrinks. And, ironically, the protective church loses more members than the church down the street that prioritizes reaching and serving the community's people. Indeed, the churches that play it safe lose more of their own children than do the missional churches. Traditional denominations lose about half of their kids by the time they have become adults; the most self-protective traditions can lose 70 percent.

Meanwhile, missional churches that reach and disciple lost people, who deploy their people in ministries and causes, whose people experience the fulfillment that comes from making a difference and being a part of something really important, thereby achieve much more member-retention than the churches that are tip-toeing into the future, buttocks first.

Churches that play not to lose often do not think of themselves that way, because they want new members; they'd like to grow and serve more people. It may even be one of the eight or ten stated goals in the church's long-range plan; but it's not their priority, and the goal is forever subordinated to protecting "our people."

Are We "Demand Siders" or "Supply Siders"?

A second major issue for their typical church decline goes deeper that the play-to-win or play-not-to-lose issue. This issue is a prominent issue in the literature of sociology of religion, but it is still foreign to most church leaders. This theory proposes two types of churches, naming them with metaphors from economics.

Many churches count on conditions in their community and society to be favorable to Christianity, conditions that encourage or stimulate people to visit churches, pray, select religious radio and television programing. or in other ways to take religious initiatives. These are **"Demand Side" churches**; they assume that whether churches flourish or flounder depends on the "demand" for religious services and experiences in the "religious marketplace." The church became all too accustomed to favorable conditions in the extended period of Christendom. Ever since, secularization and other trends that aren't on "our side" have often immobilized churches.

Other churches, however, are **"Supply Side" churches.** They take the initiative to people, and populations, on the people's turf. They know that the sower goes forth to sow the seed of God's Word on the several soils in the community. They are proactive rather than reactive. Like the apostles of old, they believe that their mission field is often "ripe for the harvest," and that the church is called to follow the Lord of the harvest into the harvest and gather it.

The obsession driving this chapter is to commend, interpret, and offer the supply side perspective to a generation of church leaders. Let's edge into that discussion with some questions to prime the pump and nuance the issues.

Essential Questions

How do the leaders of your church view the many people of your community who are not involved in any church nor register any church preference? The question is essential, because the statistical indicators tell us that there are more of them than ever before. Every county in the United States has a higher percentage of people with no reported church connection than a decade ago, many more than a generation ago.

Do you assume that everybody out there is already OK, so they do not really need what Christianity offers? Or do you assume that they are lost, like sheep without a shepherd, and they cannot find by themselves the life they deeply want and were meant for?

Do you perceive pre-Christian people as essentially a threat to the church and its people? Or is your church a local mission in their behalf?

Do you assume that, in any case, most of them cannot be reached, or would never become "real Christians" (like us) if they were reached? Or do you assume that many lost people can be found and, if reached and discipled, would produce their fair share of apostles, prophets, saints, and martyrs?

Do you assume that they "should" be Christians, and they should know that the church doors are open to them? Or do you assume that we need to understand them, identify with them, engage them, and invite them?

Do you assume that secularization is making it harder to reach lost people? Or do you assume that secularization has helped clear the way to reach lost people with a more robust expression of Christianity than they have ever been exposed to?

Two Theories of Secularization

We now know that church leaders must face such questions *everywhere*. More and more, no desirable future awaits churches anywhere if such questions are avoided. This is because we now know that the secularization of the West, which began several centuries ago, continues at an unrelenting pace; and we now know that something like secularization has impacted every industrial and postindustrial society.

Let's review, and then expand upon, what we mean by "secularization." Essentially, we mean that whole societies that were once substantially "Christian" have become substantially "secular" because institutional Christianity lost the "home-field advantage" that it enjoyed for hundreds of years. The church is now faced with a changed culture—to which churches are called to adapt or experience slow death. A sign on the office wall of E. Gordon Gee, president of Ohio State University, reads, "If you don't like change, you're going to like irrelevance even less." We widely acknowledge that something like this is true for NFL football teams, universities, governments, and all sorts of organizations, for all sorts of reasons. It is true even more for churches, but church leaders often acknowledge it less.

Locally, Christians and church leaders (who have not yet circled the wagons) keep discovering something year after year. More and more people, whose ancestors were Christians, have no idea what we Christians are even talking about. Many secular people have no Christian memory, no church to "return" to. Some functionally secular people once (say) sat through a church's catechism experience when they were children, but it did not "take"; what they once kind-of learned is now no more available to their consciousness than my high school geometry is now available to me.

The studies of secularization in the West are now so extensive that no one can read all of the literature. Broadly, and with some oversimplification, scholars now discuss two meanings that have been attached to the term "secularization."

"Secularization A," often the perspective of historians, refers to institutional Christianity's loss of the central role and influence it once enjoyed in Christendom—before sustained events like the Renaissance, the Enlightenment, and the Reformation, and the rise of Science, Nationalism, and Urbanization shifted the church's place in society from the center toward the margins. So, in this perspective, a society becomes more secular as its once-established religion loses cultural influence and loses its privileged automatic connection with most of the people.

"Secularization B" has been more often the perspective of sociologists and social theorists who have believed that as the once-established religion loses influence, most of the people become less "religious"—in *any* sense of the term; several early theorists prophesied that some societies will arrive at a time of no religion at all.

The debate is not usually about whether the A form has occurred. Most scholars find that claim undeniable. The debate is about whether the B form has occurred, and whether B necessarily follows from A. To the extent that it does follow and that societies therefore become less religious, that presents churches with a formidable challenge. Fortunately, perhaps, there was once much more support for Theory B than there is today.

The Discovery of Secularization almost Everywhere

Our awareness of secularization and its impact has expanded in recent years with the publication of sources like Pippa Norris and Ronald Inglehart's *Sacred and Secular*. Scholars like Norris (Harvard) and Inglehart (University of Michigan) are now able to demonstrate that the phenomenon of secularization is not confined to the Western societies in which churches once baptized and catechized almost everyone. Statistical data from sources like the World Values Survey now show that, worldwide, wherever formerly agrarian societies have become industrial (or postindustrial) societies, the society's predominant traditional religion—whether Animism, Hinduism, Buddhism, Islam, Shinto, Christianity or whatever—has lost influence, and the people, on average, are less religious than their forbears. (Norris and Inglehart qualify this conclusion: "Secularization is a tendency, not an iron law.")[1]

Norris and Inglehart rehearse the history of secularization theory in the writings of social theorists over the last two centuries. They feature two very useful economic metaphors to characterize more than two centuries of secularization theory within two broad perspectives.

Early social theorists, such as Durkheim, Weber, Marx, and Freud, were demand side theorists. They contended that, as societies move from agrarian life to industrial life, the people's "demand" for religion would decline. Some even predicted that secular man would no longer have any interest, much less need for, the numinous or the transcendent in any form. As one example, C. Wright Mills wrote, "Once the world was filled with the sacred—in thought, practice, and institutional form. After the Reformation and the Renaissance, the forces of modernization swept across the globe and secularization, a corollary historical process, loosened the dominance of the sacred. In due course, the sacred shall disappear altogether except, perhaps, in the private realm."[2]

Here Come the Supply Siders

Demand side theories of secularization constituted the predominant paradigm in the Western academy until the fairly late twentieth century. The most notable defector from their ranks was the sociologist Peter Berger, once a demand side guru. Berger perceived that when a society's once-predominant traditional religion loses influence, the people do *not* necessarily, or even usually, become less "religious." Other religious, philosophical, and ideological options walk in and compete for the people's devotion; secularization typically brings "religious pluralism" in its wake. So in 1999, Berger wrote, "The world today, with some exceptions . . . is as furiously religious as it ever was, and in some places more so than ever. This means that a whole body of literature by historians and social scientists labeled 'secularization theory' is essentially mistaken."[3] So Berger has distanced himself from Secularization B; he grants that Secularization A has occurred, and continues, without question.

Sociologists like Rodney Stark and Roger Finke focus gun sights upon the Secularization B paradigm that dominated for two centuries; they write not to praise early social theory's Caesars, but to bury them! "After nearly three centuries of utterly failed prophesies and misrepresentations of both present and past, it seems time to carry the secularization doctrine to the graveyard of failed theories, and there to whisper 'requiescat in pace.' "[4]

Stark and Finke, with a growing body of other thinkers, advocate a supply side theory. While they acknowledge some fluctuation in the "demand" for religion, they believe that the demand for religious identities, services, connections, and experiences is relatively constant from one generation, or age, or society to another.

Starke and Finke's perspective features two additional economic metaphors. They contend that religion tends to stagnate and lose influence in conditions of "monopoly"—such as in the European states with established churches; conversely, religion tends to thrive in social conditions that permit "competition" in a society's religious "marketplace."

Stark and Finke believe that what churches, religious organizations, and their leaders and people do in a given context is more decisive than the context in influencing whether the religion thrives and grows or stagnates and declines. The churches that take seriously, and exercise, their strategic role in serving and reaching their society tend to thrive, even in very challenging contexts—such as China; indeed, through fervent faith and strategic ministry, some churches and religious organizations become movements in very secular societies.

The supply side perspective is not without its critics. They point out that while societies with essentially a one-religion monopoly can, and often do, become societies with very low religious interest—as in Northern Europe—other such societies—such as Ireland and much of southern Europe—remain quite religious. Furthermore, while societies with religious freedom and competition can, indeed, be fairly highly religious—as in the United States, one can identify enough exceptions (one need look no farther than Canada) to lose some confidence in the theory.

Insights from the Church Growth Tradition

I believe that, while the economic metaphors are stimulating and useful, our understanding is advanced by the two generations of studies in the church growth field-research tradition within mission studies. Church growth researchers have learned that supply side strategic perspectives and actions do, indeed, contribute to a church's health, growth, and effectiveness. Admittedly, those perspectives and actions are less encouraged in the contexts where one church enjoys near monopoly, but, as in Ireland, some churches nevertheless are very missional, proactive, and entrepreneurial in outreach ministry. Likewise, while these perspectives and actions are more encouraged in an open religious marketplace, churches in competitive settings can be, and very often are, very passive, nonstrategic, demand siders—as in New Zealand.

In either a "monopoly" setting or a "competitive" setting, a church is more likely to experience a desirable future if it is aware of its theological and ministry paradigms, if it studies and adapts to its changing context, and if it finds and expresses indigenous and relevant ways to engage in ministry with people who believe and with people who do not yet believe.

To be more specific, a church in either kind of ecclesial context will engage more Christian and pre-Christian people if the church's preaching and teaching are interesting and relevant than if boring and irrelevant. The church is more likely to engage the community if its liturgy and life are expressed in ways that are indigenous to the target population's style, language, aesthetics, and music than if they experience the church as culturally alien. The church is more likely to be alive if its people are in ministry with each other in small groups than if they are mere church attendees.

Again, the church is more likely to be a local power if it regards finding lost people as its main business, rather than merely caring for the members, perpetuating the tradition, or supporting the denomination. The church is more likely to be contagious if it engages and invites lost people than if it protects its members from them *or* if it simply assumes that every baptized person in the parish is a Christian or is already OK. The church is more likely to be a local movement if its members are in ministry, if its people are inviting pre-Christian people across their friendship and kinship networks, if the church has a range of outreach ministries, if the church identifies and reaches receptive people who are "looking for life," if the members are involved in world mission far beyond the local community. The church is more "movemental" when it is proliferating new groups, new congregations, new ministries, and new outreach ministries—to engage pre-Christian people.

Such a list of specific kinds of strategic perspectives and actions that many growing churches know to engage in could be expanded. The point is that every church that regards outreach as its main business and takes a strategic approach to its planning and outreach is a supply sider church.

Scholars Can Be Clueless

Norris and Inglehart, who are unreconstructed demand siders to the core, reveal themselves to be essentially clueless in their characterization of the supply side strategy: "If you build a church, people will come."[5] That variation on a movie cliché actually fits the demand side philosophy more closely. Across much of Europe, western and eastern, the state churches have placed cathedrals and parish churches in most communities in the simple hope that people would simply come.

By comparison, supply side churches go to the people— proactively engaging pre-Christian people, in friendship and ministry, on their turf. The building of a church is merely a typical first step. Indeed, an entrepreneurial church may not wait to reach out until they can build their own facility; their first congregation may gather in a theater, a library, a pub, a hotel conference room, a school gym, or some other secular site.

So what Stark and Finke have demonstrated, I think, is that churches are less likely to think and act strategically in conditions of religious monopoly and more likely in conditions of competition. But the open context does not ensure religious vitality, and the closed context does not usually make it impossible (except in the most totalitarian homicidal societies).

Of course, the economic metaphors, like sports metaphors, have their limitations and should not be stretched too far. The category and experience of competition with other churches almost never seems to be in the minds of the leaders of the most effective churches. They are much more likely to consciously compete for people's souls and the health of the community against the forces of addiction, evil, or secularism than against other churches per se; indeed, they are increasingly likely to cooperate with other churches in a shared mission that is too much for any one church to fulfill.

Evidence of Global Secularity

Much of the Norris-Inglehart project is devoted to interpreting the global data on human religious involvement that has been more available in the last quarter-century than before. Scholars now have access to survey data from seventy-six nations, with almost five billion people, including some longitudinal data:

Religious Participation
    Collective (as in Attendance)
    Individual (as in Prayer)
Religious Values
Religious Beliefs

Norris and Inglehart interpret the data to show that generally collective and individual religious participation and the people's religious identity, values, and beliefs, have all declined as societies have moved from agrarian to industrial to postindustrial—though the decline is greater from the first transition (from agrarian to industrial) than from the second (from industrial to postindustrial).

Norris and Inglehart nuance the data and the discussion in helpful ways. For instance, they point out that the difference in religiosity between Americans and Europeans may not be as great as most scholars assume. Europeans in the past were probably not nearly as religious, on the average, as a romantic reading of Europe's glorious Christian past has assumed, so the losses have not been as enormous as the doomsayers declare. Furthermore, not as many Americans attend church as self-reported surveys indicate, because some Americans respond to surveys by saying they attend church, or vote, or read books—whether they do or not! (The number of Americans attending church in a given week may be closer to 20 percent than the 40 percent that Gallup concludes from people's self-reporting).[6]

Globally, Norris and Inglehart report two important contrasting trends that, substantially due to different birthrates in agrarian and industrial populations, now characterize the societies of the earth.[7]

1. "The publics of virtually all advanced industrial societies have been moving toward more secular orientations during the past fifty years."

   Nevertheless,

2. "The world as a whole now has more people with traditional religious views than ever before—and they constitute a growing proportion of the world's population."

The Naïve Misrepresentation of Christianity

Norris and Inglehart's most transparent agenda is to shore up the demand side paradigm in response to the supply side assault from Berger, Starke, and the others. They propose the interesting theory that "religions" essentially (and only) engage the human need for "existential security." They seem to assume that all religions are more or less the same, and they mention no other role for religion except to provide consolation for vulnerable insecure people.

The problem for religion, they believe, is that modernization and industrialization, through "human development," now contribute much more "existential security" to peoples' lives; consequently, in a "developed" society, there is less existential insecurity and therefore less need for religious services. They explain, "The most crucial precondition for security, we believe, is human development even more than purely *economic* development: it involves how far all sectors of society have equal access to schooling and literacy, basic healthcare, adequate nutrition, a clean water supply, and a minimal safety net for the needy."[8]

Norris and Inglehart believe that, generally, people without adequate food, water, health care, education, and so on are "vulnerable," so they experience "existential insecurity," and these feelings drive "religiosity."[9] So, their theory "predicts that the importance of religion in people's lives will gradually diminish with the process of human development."[10]

A View from Maslow's Hierarchy of Motives

The existential security theory has some obvious validity and it fits reasonably well with some of the data that *Sacred and Secular* features. Their theory, however, explains enormously less than they assume, and it leaves a spacious opening for strategic reflection from the Supply Side perspective.

This can be demonstrated from the most widely accepted paradigm of human motivation—as delineated in Abraham Maslow's *Motivation and Personality*.[11] Briefly, Maslow discovered that a range of motives drives people's lives, and they function in a kind of hierarchy. As lower needs are met, higher needs then drive people's lives. One can model his paradigm like this:

Self-Actualization Needs

Esteem Needs

Love and Belonging Needs

Safety Needs

Physiological Needs

So, Maslow observed, as people have sufficient food, water, and shelter, they graduate to the next level, and so on. Furthermore, Maslow observed that once people move up some on the hierarchy, they typically (but not always) experience Aesthetic Needs and Worldview Needs they had not experienced before. So one can model his full paradigm like this:

Worldview Needs

Aesthetic Needs

Self-Actualization Needs

Esteem Needs

Love and Belonging Needs

Safety Needs

Physiological Needs

The Norris-Inglehart theory assumes that the human needs relevant to religion only exist when people are at the lowest levels on the hierarchy. Once people have food, water, health care, educations, and so on, they are "developed," and have graduated from a need-driven life orientation. Maslow observed, however, that people at the midlevels and even the higher levels are by no means completed humans; they are now driven for healthier self-esteem or a satisfying worldview or for self-fulfillment.

The existential security theory of religion also assumes that religion can only help people who feel vulnerable—at Maslow's lower levels. (Unfortunately, too much religious practice reflects that limited paradigm; too many churches seem to offer only consolation for the tears and terrors in this life and heaven for the next.)

However, the strategic churches that know to adjust to people who have adequate nutrition, healthcare, and education, who help people discover their identity and purpose as Christ-followers and experience the aesthetic power in the church's liturgy, music, and arts, and view life and the world through the lenses of a New Testament worldview, will gather harvests in the very places that some of the social theorists assume that "religion," by definition, has nothing to offer the people anymore.

Christianity is a redemptive approach to life as a whole, and to the whole person (and to whole societies). The church is entrusted with the ministries of *kerygma* (the message), *didache* (the ethical teachings), *leitourgia* (worship), *koinonia* (fellowship), and *diakonia* (ministry)— which, together, engage every human need on Maslow's hierarchy.

Church leaders who think this through, making the visual connections, will be empowered with a more comprehensive understanding of what the Christian faith offers people. To that end, I invite you to list, in a column, the general human needs (or clusters of needs) that Abraham Maslow discovered:

Physiological needs

Safety needs

Love and Belonging needs

Esteem (from self and others) needs

Self-actualization needs

Aesthetic needs

Worldview needs

Continue, in that column, to list some other human needs for which, we have discovered, Christianity is relevant and redemptive. People often express their needs as questions, like:

Who am I?

What is the meaning of life?

What is the purpose of my life?

How do I justify, or validate, my life?

How do I experience real life?

How can I hope to experience life after death?

How does God want me to live my life?

How can my life make a difference?

What kind of hope is there for this world?

Now, to the right of those two lists combined, list the general resources of the Gospel:

Kerygma

Didache

Leitourgia

Koinonia

Diakonia

Now start making the connections, from your own Christian studies, experience, and imagination. I will get you started. Christianity can help meet some of people's "lower" needs, such as for food, clothing or shelter, as Christians exercise ministries of diakonia; Christians experience some of their own needs being met—such as the need for purpose, the need to make a difference, and the need for self-actualization—as a by-product of giving themselves in diakonia.

Some of the data from the Norris-Inglehart project virtually broadcasts opportunity for an adaptive missional faith that the authors, with their limited understanding of Christianity's nature and relevance, miss in toto. They report that the people's survey data from eighteen out of twenty industrial or postindustrial countries report a recent twenty-year "rise in thinking about the meaning of life."[12] As Dean Kelley once reminded us,[13] the question that Christianity is most intended to answer is, What is the Meaning of Life?

So one objective of serious Christian mission is to raise people into sufficient existential security that they can become open to the questions that the gospel was most sent to address.

Strategic churches, with a supply side perspective, are called and commissioned to offer and interpret the gospel in every society's religious marketplace because, as Leander Keck noted, "The gospel is the only thing we have to offer the world that it does not already have." They engage in mission believing that the Holy Spirit has prepared many people's hearts for good news and life change, that many people will be receptive if we reach out in appropriate ways, that deep down people are hungering for the truth, reality, healing, and life that God offers through the gospel, Christian experience, and Christian community.

We have known, in the church growth research tradition, not to deny or minimize what Norris-Inglehart call the demand side perspective. We know, from extensive mission data and experience that, at a given time, some societies and populations are relatively "resistant," while other societies and populations are relatively "receptive." C. Peter Wagner once demonstrated that it is possible to position each target population at some point along a "Resistance-Receptivity Axis."[14] Here is one version:

Hostility—Resistance—Indifference—Receptiveness—Readiness

We have observed that, over time, receptivity "ebbs and flows" along that axis and that there are many contributing causes of people becoming more or less receptive; industrialization and human development are only two of more than a dozen known causes. Strategically, we have known to especially reach out to receptive people and populations *while they are receptive*—knowing that the conditions that now contribute to their openness will not last forever.

Strategic churches have also known not to abandon resistant populations, but rather to establish and maintain a loving presence among them. Indeed, we have learned that the ministry of presence helps plants the seeds of a harvest that will come later, in God's good time.

Furthermore, Christian leaders and people in the tradition of the apostles have never been intimidated by the possibility that the current "demand" for religion might be low. St. Patrick, William Carey, and J. Hudson Taylor did not wait for official invitations from Ireland, India, or China to begin their missions.

AFTERWORD:
CHOOSING
YOUR FUTURE

One year, my wife and I spent a wonderful two weeks leading seminars for Salvation Army leaders in New Zealand. The nation was then hosting a major international rugby football tournament. It was a big deal. Every Kiwi was rooting for New Zealand's beloved All Blacks.

In the evenings, the rugby tournament dominated the television channels, so we watched rugby matches. It is an exciting game, like hyper-caffeinated American football on steroids. I gradually inferred some of the game's rules. Apparently, for instance, players can pass the ball backward or laterally, but forward passes are not permitted.

One Salvation Army officer in our large group had once been a star player for the All Blacks, and he had then served as the team's defense coach before entering the army's service. One day I asked him, "What would happen if a rule change permitted the forward pass?" He reflected for several minutes before commenting, "That would change every team's game plan. It would take time to rethink how the game would now be played. The team that figured it out first would have an enormous advantage."

The church in the West, in the last five hundred years and the last fifty years, has experienced many game-changing events at least that big. This book has reported several of the major changes in the "field" in which the church is placed:

1. The Western world has become substantially secular.

2. More and more people in the West are secular people.

3. More and more secular people are also postmodern people.

4. The church no longer enjoys a religious monopoly in Western society.

5. The church does not live, anymore, in a privileged position within the society.

6. The community surrounding every church has become a secular mission field.

Granting such facts, an apostolic congregation's identity includes these themes:

a. The church is called to be an apostolate even more than an ecclesia.

b. The church's main business is to serve as God's mission in the world.

c. This mission is primarily entrusted to the laity, whose sphere of influence is the world.

We have also especially reflected upon three features of a mission strategy for secular Western mission fields:

7. The people of God are best deployed in mission in the world in teams.

8. To be effective in a game that changes from time to time, the strategic church is a serious learning organization—

eager to learn from Scripture, tradition, relevant academic fields, statistical data, and from pioneering churches.

9. While the strategic church takes the demand side realities seriously, nevertheless it dreams, plans, and engages in proactive outreach ministry from a supply side strategic perspective.

Alas, this book does not presume to cover all that can be known about being the church in mission in our time. But I can commend several other books that represent additional insight that many church leaders will need.

10. Long range strategic planning is indispensable for serious churches in any mission field. I have exposed readers to versions of what a strategic plan might look like in *To Spread the Power* and *The Apostolic Congregation*.[1]

11. More is now known about how the faith spreads and how churches grow than we have ever known before. *To Spread the Power* and *The Apostolic Congregation* are my two contributions to local mission strategy.

12. This book only addresses the ministry of evangelism in parts of two chapters. Several of my books teach more evangelism than this one: *To Spread the Power, How to Reach Secular People, Church for the Unchurched, Radical Outreach,* and *The Apostolic Congregation* each devote a chapter to some of what is known about how we help pre-Christian people to experience faith and become Christ-followers.[2] My *Celtic Way of Evangelism* draws from the most sustained premodern Christian mission to exhibit approaches to reaching postmodern people today.[3]

13. Since missional Christianity hopes to experience local Christian movements everywhere, we might learn from the leadership and strategic perspectives of other social movements. *The Recovery of a Contagious Methodist Movement* unpacks this possibility.[4]

I need to conclude by featuring the power of the pivotal choices that church leaders sometimes make. After all, a church's present and future are substantially shaped by the major decisions once made by the church's forbears. For example, if you worship and serve in a long-established church, the decision makers who once designed your sanctuary now influence your life every week. That planning group may now be deceased, but their decisions still influence who might be attracted to the church and who might not, what kinds of services and programs the sanctuary can handle, who can hear what from where, and so on.

There are some major decisions you probably get to make only once. The church will be experiencing the trade-offs from those decisions for as long as it exists. Some decisions will deeply affect whether you reach new people or simply care for the existing congregation.

Take, for instance, the issue of location. The folk wisdom around new church planting says that the three most important issues in planting a new church are "location, location, and location." Where you choose to locate a church can speak volumes about your church's identity and how it understands its main business. Where you choose to locate a church can announce the kind of future you want the church to have—which, of course, is the substantial issue; almost any location will have advantages and disadvantages.

Imagine yourself in the following historical case study—based loosely on an actual case (with some historical fiction added).

It is late winter 1871. In six weeks you will ride the stagecoach to become the pastor of a brand new church in Shiloh—a fairly new town in western Kansas. The first settlers arrived to constitute the town soon after the United States government opened the territory to settlement seventeen years ago; Kansas became a state ten years ago. The mayor (and general store proprietor) has informed you, in correspondence, that almost eight hundred people live in or near the town, with farms and small settlements beyond.

A block of stores already line the main street, behind the raised boarded sidewalks, with hitching posts in front. The stores include a Wells Fargo bank, a stagecoach depot, telegraph office, post office, a restaurant with hotel rooms upstairs, the marshall's office and jail, a blacksmith and gunsmith, a hardware and feed store, a doctor's office and six-bed clinic, a barber who also does some dentistry, the general store, and the Firewater Saloon. A small schoolhouse stands on the east edge of town. This summer, a grocery and pharmacy will replace the open-air tented farmers market. Other shops and offices are planned; Shiloh's mayor reports that the people are clamoring for "a real dentist!"

Although Shiloh is a biblical name, the town does not yet have a church. Your denomination has usually been much earlier to plant churches in frontier towns. The mayor reports that people in the town are so eager to have a church that two different two-acre lots (one acre for the chapel, one for a cemetery) have been reserved for a new church to choose from. Ten families have already been meeting and asking for a pastor; if a new pastor will join them, they want him to choose the lot for the church.

The mayor says they need for you to choose a lot now so that three stores and offices can build on the other land this summer. One of the two-acre lots is at the edge of town, across from the schoolhouse. The other is in the middle of town, with the bank on one side, the marshall's office and jail on the other, and the Firewater Saloon across the street.

How would your letter to the mayor respond to the town's generous offer? Which lot would you choose? Why? Your decision reflects your philosophy of ministry, your priorities, your vision, and your understanding of your new church's main business. Furthermore, your decision will influence who your church will be most likely to reach and serve, and least likely to reach and serve. (Your decision will also reflect your understanding of your calling—as either a chaplain or an apostle.)

In the actual case upon which this scenario is based, the pastor and his nucleus of believers chose the lot in the middle of town. They "loved on" the town and its people; they conversed with the people on the wooden sidewalks and sometimes prayed with them; except for winters, the people could overhear the celebration, the singing, the preaching, and the prayers through the church's open door and windows.

Several of the members especially befriended Ed, whose horse was often observed hitched in front of the saloon. One day, people saw his horse hitched in front of the church, and the next day, and the next. When people asked him why, he said, "I changed hitching posts!" Ed became familiar with sobriety and sanity, he ceased picking fights and abusing his wife and children, and the whole family became disciples. Several Firewater buddies became involved and their families and neighbors. Several men and women from the jail and their families and friends were also reached. The church became a local movement. Many of Shiloh's regular people, beyond the ten families who were first involved, were attracted to the miracles. The church that "civilized" Shiloh became legendary.

Meanwhile, in surrounding towns, most of the other churches chose a safer path. To this day, they are small struggling congregations who take care of their own. Occasionally, they experience the impulse or the obligation to become fishers of men and women, but the only fish they really want to catch are the fish that have already been cleaned.

NOTES

1. How the Game Changed

1. Martin Marty, *The Modern Schism: Three Paths to the Secular* (London: SCM Press, 1969).

2. Hendrik Kraemer, *A Theology of the Laity* (Vancouver, BC: Regent College Publishing, 2005), 186.

3. Charles Taylor, *A Secular Age* (Cambridge, MA: Belknap Press of Harvard University Press, 2007), 2.

4. Donald O. Soper, *The Advocacy of the Gospel* (Nashville: Abingdon, 1961).

5. See http://blogs.the-american-interest.com/berger/2012/07/03/the-koran-and-historical-scholarship/.

6. See Leonard Sweet, *Post-Modern Pilgrims: First Century Passion for the 21st Century Church* (Nashville: B&H Books, 2000).

2. The Once and Future Christian Lay Movement

1. You can see films of the King and His Court performing on YouTube. Once on YouTube's site, enter "King and His Court softball." Be sure to watch the black and white newsreel footage of 1959.

2. When Feigner was pitching blindfolded, the umpire called almost anything he could see a "Strike!"

3. Hendrik Kraemer, *A Theology of the Laity* (1958; repr., Vancouver: Regent College Publishing, 2005).

4. Ibid., 47.

5. Ibid., 55.

6. Ibid., 50.

7. Ibid., 68–69.

8. Richard Baxter, *The Reformed Pastor*, ed. William Brown (Carlisle, PA: Banner of Truth Trust, 1974).

9. Kraemer, *A Theology of the Laity*, 127–28.
10. Ibid., 128.
11. Ibid., 130–31.

3. Missional Christianity Is a "Team Game"

1. Warren Bennis, *Leaders: Strategies of Taking Charge*, 2nd ed. (New York: HarperBusiness, 1997).

2. From this team perspective, choosing people with the requisite expertise is a crucial step in developing a team. If you are the pastor, and you know children's ministry, youth ministry, recovery ministry, music ministry, and so on better than the people with those responsibilities, you have populated the would-be team with the wrong people!

3. Wagner's first text, from the 1980s, *Your Spiritual Gifts Can Help Your Church Grow*, was republished by Regal Books in 2012. *Discover Your Spiritual Gifts* (Ventura, CA: Regal, 2012) is his latest contribution to this type of resource.

4. The seminar guidebook is now published. See Eric Rees, *S.H.A.P.E.: Finding and Fulfilling Your Unique Purpose for Life* (Grand Rapids: Zondervan, 2006). The book additionally provides access to a free online S.H.A.P.E. assessment.

5. Some of these questions were suggested, years ago, by Ray Bakke's *The Urban Christian* (Downers Grove, IL: IVP Academic, 1987).

6. I have developed the eight steps, adapting from the courses of the American Management Association, in George G. Hunter III, *Leading and Managing a Growing Church* (Nashville: Abingdon Press, 2000). The book's usefulness is not limited to the leaders of churches that are already growing. It shows that the effective management of a church, as an organization with a distinctive purpose, is one demonstrable path to growth. (From another perspective, the leaders of stagnant and declining churches are usually neglecting one or more of these steps.) Consider one of the steps: planning. I have never found a church that had an *informed* strategic plan, *owned* by the people, informing every major *decision*, and being regularly *implemented* that was not growing. Growing churches typically plan their work and then work their plan.

4. Who (or What) Will We Learn From?

1. Reported in Robert H Waterman, Jr., *The Renewal Factor: How to Best Get and Keep the Competitive Edge* (New York: Bantam Books: 1987), 111.

2. See Grace Reese, *Unbinding the Gospel: Real Life Evangelism*, 2nd ed. (St. Louis: Chalice, 2011) and *Unbinding Your Heart: 40 Days of Prayer and Faith Sharing* (St. Louis: Chalice, 2008) for some of the more innovative recent literature on evangelism.

3. The rest of this chapter is an adaptation of my article, "Megachurches" in *The Encyclopedia of Protestantism*, vol. 3, (New York: Routledge, 2004).

4. Peter F. Drucker, *The Age of Discontinuity: Guidelines to Our Changing Society* (New York: Harper and Row, 1968), 173.

5. Angelus Temple was designed by William H. Wheeler, the brilliant architect of the most notable West Coast theaters of the time, who designed the church with unprecedented acoustics and with two balconies that permitted the preacher to engage a ground floor attendance of 1,000 to 1,200 plus two "stacked" congregations of 800 to 1,000 in each balcony. Spurgeon's Tabernacle featured two wrap-around balconies in addition to the ground-floor congregation. Both McPherson's and Spurgeon's large churches featured several services each weekend, which enabled the total attendance for which they are legendary today. Those churches, however, were exceptions and were not within the experience of most Protestant Christians and leaders. And even some apparent exceptions were not so exceptional after all. People who tour Europe sometimes reply that many famous churches in Europe—like St. Paul's in London and St. Peter's in Rome—were built centuries ago and are enormous even by today's standards. True, but the actual seating area for a congregation usually accommodates only 500 to 1,200 people, and the agenda was less on the homily and more on liturgy, choral music, and pageantry, which have a greater reliable range than the unaided speaking voice.

6. This is a descriptive observation. Some megachurches, by their policy, do not receive people by "transfer" from other churches; they count all new members as "converts"—whether they are or not! In church growth lore, however, if people were active members of a church before they joined the megachurch, we classify all such growth as transfer growth.

7. These are among the strategic themes in my books *To Spread the Power: Church Growth in the Wesleyan Spirit* (Nashville: Abingdon, 1987) and *The Apostolic Congregation: Church Growth Reconceived for a New Generation* (Abingdon, 2010).

8. There may be an occasional exception. If a pastor leads the worship and preaches, leads the choir and takes up the offering, teaches all the Sunday school classes, leads all the groups, and opens up, cleans up, and locks up, and does all the office work and all of the "shepherding,"—that pastor is not a manager; but if anyone but the pastor does any of that, some management is involved.

9. One book that repeats the party-line charges that megachurches follow church growth, management, and marketing principles is Elaine A. Robinson, *Godbearing: Evangelism Reconceived* (Cleveland: Pilgrim Press, 2006). The book is rife with slogans like "the managerial mindset."

10. See Norman Shawchuck, Philip Kotler, and Bruce Wrenn, *Marketing for Congregations: Choose to Serve People More Effectively* (Nashville: Abingdon, 1992).

11. I have delineated this marketing approach in much greater detail, with case studies in *To Spread the Power: Church Growth in the Wesleyan Spirit* (Nashville: Abingdon, 1987), 131–50.

12. See "Does Megachurch 'High' Explain Their Success?", www.realclearreligion.org/.../getting_high_at_a_megachurch_249530.htm

13. A. H. Maslow, *Religions, Values, and Peak Experiences* (Toronto: Penguin Books Canada, Limited, 1983).

14. See my book, *The Apostolic Congregation: Church Growth Reconceived for a New Generation* (Nashville: Abingdon Press; 2010), 55–60, for a more thorough discussion of religious affections, including the theory of The Sublime and some implications for mission, evangelism, and worship.

15. See Greg L. Hawkins and Cally Parkinson, *Reveal: Where Are You?* (South Barrington, IL: Willow Creek Association, 2007).

16. Philip Jenkins, *God's Continent: Christianity, Islam and Europe's Religious Crisis* (New York: Oxford University Press, 2007).

17. For much more on megachurches, see Lynne and Bill Hybels: *Rediscovering Church: The Story and Vision of Willow Creek Community Church* (Grand Rapids: Zondervan, 1995); Donald E. Miller, *Reinventing American Protestantism* (Berkeley: University of California Press, 1997); Lyle Schaller, *The Seven-Day-a-Week-Church* (Nashville: Abingdon, 1992) and *The Very Large Church* (Nashville: Abingdon, 2000); Scott Thumma, Dave Travis, and Rick Warren, *Beyond Megachurch Myths: What We Can Learn from America's Largest Churches* (San Francisco: Jossey-Bass, 2007); and Rick Warren, *The Purpose Driven Church* (Grand Rapids: Zondervan, 1995).

5. A "Supply Side" Response to Secularization Everywhere

1. Pippa Norris and Ronald Inglehart, *Sacred and Secular: Religion and Politics Worldwide*, 2nd ed. (Cambridge, UK: Cambridge University Press, 2011), 5. Nor, I would add, is secularity the same everywhere; it typically takes a different shape in a post-Animist, pos-Shinto, post-Buddhist, or even a post-communist society, than in a Western post-Christian society.

2. C. Wright Mills, *The Sociological Imagination* (Oxford: Oxford University Press), 32–33, quoted in Norris and Inglehart, *Sacred and Secular*, 3.

3. Peter I. Berger, ed., *The Desecularization of the World* (Washington, DC: Ethics and Public Policy Center, 1999), 2, quoted in Norris and Inglehart, *Sacred and Secular*, 4.

4. Rodney Stark and Roger Finke, *Acts of Faith* (Berkeley, CA: University of California Press, 1999), 79, quoted in Norris and Inglehart, *Sacred and Secular*.

5. Norris and Inglehart, *Sacred and Secular*, 7.

6. There are other ways to contrast the relevant differences between Europe and North America. Norris and Inglehart might have reported that in contrast to Americans, many Europeans under-report their religious involvement in face-to-face surveys. They might also have reported that one reason why European churches are seen by American visitors to be much less full than American churches is that while most American churches are built to accommodate their Sunday-by-Sunday attendance, most European churches were built to accommodate their (still large) Easter and Christmas Eve attendance. Furthermore, when their surveys ask if, in the past week, people have attended church other than attending a baptism, wedding, or funeral, the resulting data obscure the fact that Europeans generally attend

baptisms, weddings, and funerals much more often than Americans do—which puts Europeans in church more often than the data on Sunday church attendance reveals.

7. Norris and Inglehart, *Sacred and Secular,* 5.

8. Ibid., 55.

9. Ibid., 4.

10. Ibid., 56.

11. Abraham Maslow, *Motivation and Personality,* rev. ed. (New York: Harper and Brothers, 1954; Joanna Cotler Books, 1970).

12. Norris and Inglehart, *Sacred and Secular,* 75.

13. See Dean M. Kelley, *Why Conservative Churches Are Growing* (New York: Harper and Row, 1972).

14. See C. Peter Wagner, *Strategies for Church Growth* (Ventura, CA: Regal, 1987).

Afterword: Choosing Your Future

1. See George G. Hunter III, *To Spread the Power: Church Growth in the Wesleyan Spirit* (Nashville: Abingdon, 1987), chap. 8; and *The Apostolic Congregation: Church Growth Reconceived for a New Generation* (Nashville: Abingdon, 2010), chap. 7.

2. George G. Hunter III, *To Spread the Power,* chap. 4; *How To Reach Secular People* (Nashville: Abingdon, 1992), chap. 3; *Church for the Unchurched* (Nashville: Abingdon, 1996), chap. 6; *Radical Outreach: The Recovery of Apostolic Ministry and Evangelism* (Nashville: Abingdon, 2003), ch. 7; *The Apostolic Congregation,* chap. 6.

3. Hunter, *The Celtic Way of Evangelism: How Christianity Can Reach the West . . . Again,* rev. ed. (Nashville: Abingdon, 2000, 2010).

4. Hunter, *The Recovery of a Contagious Methodist Movement* (Nashville: Abingdon, 2011), especially chaps. 2 and 3.

CPSIA information can be obtained at www.ICGtesting.com
Printed in the USA
LVOW100313260313

325955LV00003B/4/P